Home Grown in Cumbria

Annette Gibbons

with photographs by

James Walker

Zymurgy
Publishing

© Text - Annette Gibbons
© Images - James Walker

Design: Nick Ridley

Printed by MKT Print and Compass Press Ltd

First published 2005 by Zymurgy Publishing, Newcastle upon Tyne, United Kingdom

A catalogue record for this book is available from the British Library.

10 9 8 7 6 5 4 3 2 1

I.S.B.N. 1-903506-15-8

This book is being part financed by the European Agricultural Guidance and Guarantee
Fund of the European Union and the Department for Environment Food and Rural
Affairs through the Cumbria Fells and Dales LEADER + Programme.
The programme assists businesses and organisations involved with 'adding value to local
products' and has assisted the development of the vibrant local produce economy featured
in this book.

Contents

Baking 5
Dairy 11
Vegetables 23
Pork 33
Beef 41
Herdwick Sheep 45
Venison 51
Sausages 57
Brown Shrimps 63
Beer 69
Fruit 75
Fresh Water Fish 83
Wild Boar 91

Recipes

Starters, Preserves & Salads 96
Main Course 111
Vegetables 127
Puddings & Cakes 137
Bread 148

Appendix 155

Introduction

This is an exciting time to be involved with food in Cumbria. For the past twenty-five years I have had a keen interest in what is grown and reared here, and watched with delight as the range of foods has increased and developed. Good food has always been available in Cumbria, but we now have more people in the county producing meat with flavour, sausages with texture, traditional preserves, and hand-crafted butter and cheese. These people are enthusiastic, keen and committed to the foods they produce. They supply vegetables grown to suit their environment, that taste how vegetables should. They lavish time and care on the animals that they rear, and produce meat with great flavour. They grind flour from grains grown for the best taste. 'Quality not quantity' is an adage I grew up with. The real food being produced by these growers and farmers is the food that interests me, and I have been out to visit people to see what they do, and how they do it, while caring for the glorious Cumbrian countryside.

Home Grown in Cumbria is a snapshot of 'what's what and who's who' in good food in the county, with recipes for you to try. I am a professional cook, not a chef, and have the health of everybody at the heart of my recipes. I'm happy to spend good money on good food, and would like to encourage others to do the same so that the very best local food is cooked simply and enjoyed by all. I've included a section on where to buy good Cumbrian food and although this is a large county, I hope there will be somewhere close to you.

Eating is such a pleasure, to be enjoyed and shared. I hope you will enjoy learning about the people who produce good Cumbrian food, and that you will create your own versions of my recipes.

Annette

To Alex and Laura for being enthusiastic and especially to Paul who's always there for me.

I dedicate this book to Paul.

Baking

There's been a tradition of home baking in Cumbria for many years and it survives today. Although wheat hasn't always been grown widely in the county, unlike oats and barley and a little bit of rye, the baking of bread, cakes, scones, puddings and pastries have been an important daily occurrence for centuries. The skills needed and utensils used have changed over time as methods of cooking have developed but on the whole recipes have been passed down through generations.

After the Romans, Viking and Norse settlers arrived around the 9th century and brought with them the word 'haver' (hafre is Norse for oats). Most farmers who grew oats would have it milled and dried in kilns locally and then returned to them to be stored in oak kists placed in a warm and dry position, often upstairs within the house. These chests for storing oats were known as haver kists and were still in use along the Solway coast up to the nineteen fiftees.

From the seventeenth century onwards haver bread, also known as clap bread, was put onto a bakboard or clap board which was a round piece of wood with a concave top which helped to drive the dough into shape before baking. The haver bread was baked on a 'baekstein' or bake stone which was constructed upon a brick furnace, fired with juniper wood, which was readily available and of such quality that it gave off little ash. The stone was heated up sufficiently to bake large numbers of breads at any one time. The breads were possibly up to a yard in diameter and became smaller as girdles were produced to cook breads on open fires.

Around the same time there were groups of itinerant workers (mostly women) who were 'professional' cooks who would spend time at each outlying farm baking bread. After cooking, this flat bread was dried and stored and the women would stay until enough bread was made to last the family six months before moving on to the next farm.

Baking in Cumbria has given rise to a number of different breads, cakes and pastries which take their names from the villages where they were prepared. Hawkshead Wiggs, which can still be bought in the village of Hawkshead, and are rolls made with an enriched dough sometimes including dried fruit.

Sweet breads, biscuits and tarts also reflect the geography in the county, Borrowdale Teabread, Grasmere Gingerbread, Cumberland Rum Nicky being traditional Cumbrian specialities. The influence of the trade coming into the west Cumbrian ports is reflected in the use of spices such as ginger, pepper, nutmeg, rum, and sugar. Sadly this connection derives from the slave trade at a time when slaves from Africa were being sent to the West Indies, from where the spices were traded back to Cumbria and yarns, cloths and Herdwick fleeces were then sent to Africa.

At different times of the year cakes and pastries would be made to celebrate, just as today we have a very rich fruity Christmas or wedding cake, a buttery Simnel cake and spicy hot cross buns for Easter.

Farming folk had cakes and pastries for specific events in the agricultural calendar, Clipping Time Pudding and Crundle Pudding (made with the rich first milk of a cow after it had calved) being two such dishes. Stepmother's Tart reflects the ingredients used (again spices and fruit) but this time using many different ingredients – as many as the people that a stepmother has to deal with in an extended family! Then there's Cumberland courting cake, which when offered to a prospective son-in-law, he should only eat if his intentions towards the daughter are

honourable. And Fidget Pie that contains smoked bacon, apple, sage and eggs which settle in the pastry and 'fidget'. before going into the oven.

Most commercial bakeries use the 'Chorleywood Process' which was introduced in the mid-1960s. The process uses high-speed mixing to agitate the dough and steam to reduce the time required for dough to rise. Allowing time for dough to rise develops texture and flavour. Large scale bread manufacture usually uses flour with 'added improvers' milled to perform well in factory conditions.

Andrew Whitley of Bread Matters fame initiated the Village Bakery at Melmerby in the 1970s constructing a wood fired oven to create the textures and flavours of breads from his youth. He started by researching the local history of breadmaking. Andrew tells the story of interviewing a William Dodd of Ousby who was then aged 80. William remembered in the time around 1910 going out into the fields to work but stopping for "Ten O'Clocks" which was a "slice of Barley Bannock, a large flat round bread that wasn't big enough to share, eaten with a Willimoor Whang", the strange name given to a local hard cheese from the Frizington area.

Dave Harris Jones, miller

The story of Ana and Nick Jones at The Watermill in Little Salkeld begins in 1974 when they took over the mill. Then it was just ticking over milling cattle feed for local farmers after two hundred years

The water wheel at Little Salkeld

of flour making. The 18th century mill appeared to be destined for housing until Ana and Nick fell in love with it. The milling machinery was all in place including the flour stones which although they hadn't been used for many years were still viable.

Ana first tasted wholemeal bread when she was sixteen and remembers afterwards that this was the only bread she ever wanted to eat. "It was unlike any I had ever tasted; nutty, with a wonderful texture and of course very filling." Their aim was to produce stoneground flour

The sacks of stone ground flour are raised aloft

from English wheat and bake delicious scones, cakes and bread with it. "When Nick and I lived at Lamplugh near Whitehaven my Dad would bring us sacks of organic Yorkshire wheat which we ground in our hand coffee grinder – so really a watermill was the next stage!"

The water for the mill comes from Sunnygill Beck which flows from Cross Fell, the highest part of the Pennines in the Eden Valley. As it is usually raining or snowing on the top there's always a good source of water to turn the iron and steel wheels. Originally the waterwheels would have had wooden paddles but they were replaced in 1917. There is a weir at the top of the millrace whereby on raising a sluice gate they can control the flow of water. Another stream called Little Beck joins the race and this can have enough water in it to fill the race and more. As a result of this, the Joneses are more aware of the weather than most people and have to go up to race to shut the sluice in the worst of weathers and even in the middle of the night if it has rained hard on the Pennines and the beck has filled up. The larger of the two waterwheels is housed in the wheel house and produces the power which turns the French Burr stones in the mill. This waterwheel would also have run sandstone stones that milled very coarsely for animal feed. The smaller wheel was put in during the 19th century when the mill was doubled in size and had the Granary put on the top.

The great difference between stoneground flour and other flour is the method of milling. At the mill the flour is poured into a hopper which gently feeds it between the French Burr stones. These stones are quarried from the outskirts of Paris and are said to produce the best flour in the world. Stone grinding is a more gentle process than using stainless steel rollers, keeping more of the natural texture.

The Joneses had help from a millwright to enable them to get the French Burr millstones milling again. The pieces of stone are cemented together and then bound with iron bands. They have to be taken up and sharpened every couple of years as the two grinding surfaces work rather like scissors: they cut the grain near the centre of the stone and then it is ground much finer towards the edge of the stones. The grain takes just a few seconds to be ground, and then thrown out from the stones and falls down a chute into a sack below as 100% wholemeal flour.

Milling by stone doesn't refine the flour to the same extent as stainless steel rollers and this is reflected in the taste and texture of the finished flour.

Ana and Nick have been organic millers and gardeners for nearly thirty years and are now biodynamic. They have two farmers who grow most of their wheat, rye and spelt in Kent and Leicestershire. They have always milled British grain as they consider it to be very tasty and to makes an excellent loaf. I am always impressed by their knowledge of the actual grain right down to the fact that they know the variety of each grain they mill. As each harvest is cropped they take small samples and revert to the coffee grinder technique of milling the wheat and baking with it to find out what the real flavour will be. From their results they decide upon which variety to take that year. Their commitment to flavour and quality is outstanding and their flour is a delight to use.

Dairy

Cumbria is a dairy county. Cumbria has more dairy cows than anywhere in Britain apart from Devon and more than the whole of Scotland. Sheep as well as cows have been milked here since monastic times with butter having been made for local consumption. The old counties of Cumberland and Westmorland which today make up Cumbria, never were big cheese counties; butter was the order of the day since farmers preferred milk to be made into butter from the cream, leaving skimmed milk for feeding to calves. Cheese-making however produces whey as a by-product which was only good enough to feed pigs, which were not kept in large numbers. It is only in the last twenty five years that flavoursome and well-textured cheeses have come to the fore.

Early in the 19th century Longhorn cattle were indigenous to the old counties of Cumberland and Westmorland. They were not found to be a particularly good breed for dairy use and Shorthorn cattle were developed which produced a better quality milk. Penrith was the main market in the country for buying Shorthorn; indeed Cumberland and Westmorland had their own herd book registered in Penrith and the town was recognised as a centre of excellence for the breed.

At a time when most homesteads in Cumberland and Westmorland had dairy cows for their own consumption, the arrival of the Lancaster and Carlisle railway in 1846 led to farmers gaining access to markets in towns. In fact most farms were within ten miles of a station. Incredibly in 1860 farms in the area around Mardale (the valley which was flooded in the 1930s to create the reservoir of Haweswater) were sending three thousand pounds (in weight) of butter a week to Manchester. At this time cream was removed from the top of the milk each day using a brass skimmer and may have been stored for a week until enough was ready to be made into butter. The taste of butter from that period would differ greatly from the fresh butter we now expect.

From 1875 railways also opened up agriculture in the new world and our markets were flooded with imports of wheat and meat products. This led to a focus on dairy farming.

Surprisingly cheese was imported into England at this time from America. Agricultural émigrés had taken their rural skills to North America, where women who had been instrumental in the manufacture of cheese successfully aided in the construction of manufacturing plant and export of dairy products. At that time most butter came from Normandy or Holland. Between 1860 and 1910 home production of cheese fell by two thirds and butter by only a little less, against a backcloth of rising consumption and growing population.

Records show however that The London and North West Railway Company carried 540 tons of butter from Cumberland and Westmorland stations between 1891-1892, so perhaps local butter production was still going strong.

Another surprising turn of events happened in the 1880s. The Temperance Movement attempted to reduce the number of licensed premises, to discourage the use of alcohol that was obviously affecting the workforce. The money paid as compensation for the licensees was in fact syphoned off to the local council who intelligently invested in a migratory dairy school. This consisted initially of one man or woman, the dairy instructress and three or four horses depending on the terrain they needed to cover, a tent with a slatted floor, mechanical separators and up to date hygiene equipment. They were able to travel around educating people in the procedures of butter-making. Canon Rawnsley of Keswick was instrumental in the development of the migratory dairy school which he inaugurated at Keswick.

At the same time Aspatria Agricultural College developed a dairy with Carricks of Low Row near Brampton that had been established as the first butter factory in England. Their retail outlets were on the east coast where a larger urban population lived and which was connected by the railway. The building still stands; it used to be a bus station and is now a garage.

Another historical building with a connection to the counties' dairy industry is J. & J Graham's in Penrith which was built to blend local butter. People in Cumberland and Westmorland had difficulty in producing butter of sufficiently consistent quality, as their premises were not up to standard, so it was blended to produce a uniform product.

In 1933 the Milk Marketing Board was initiated. Ironically the following year Nestle's factory in Dalston cancelled the farming contracts overnight. A Miss Ball from Newton Rigg, the Agricultural College near Penrith, acquired portable cheese-making equipment and gained access to The Mill at Warwick Bridge

The curd was suspended in the whey. The whey has been siphoned off to feed to the calves. The curd settles into large chunks which Eric turns to allow the excess whey to drain

The curds are now hand milled and salted

The milled curds are mixed by hand

The milled cheese is put into blue lined cheese moulds before being pressed

where local school children from the Brampton area and students from Newton Rigg used the farmers' milk to make cheese.

People today still remember local butter makers selling their fresh home-made butter in the market in Carlisle in the 1960s.

A low point in Cumbria's dairy history was in the 1970s, when the Border Dairy in Shaddongate, Carlisle, was producing butter that was sent to Ireland to be repacked and returned as Kerrygold!

Today Cumbria can boast one artisan butter maker and two artisan farmhouse cheese makers including the unpasteurised Birdoswald cheese.

Slack House Farm Birdoswald Cheese

Eric and Dianne Horn are the only organic cheese-makers in the county. Both are Yorkshire born and bred from farming stock, but in 1995 they decided to escape what they describe as the 'rambling urbanisation of West Yorkshire'. It doesn't get much more rural than Slack House Farm situated overlooking Birdoswald Fort on Hadrian's Wall away from any busy road. The word 'slack' means a wet hollow and this Cumbrian dialect describes the field in front of their house exactly.

The farm had previously been in one family for over two hundred years and they only had twelve cows. The family wanted to retire but decided

Each cheese is pressed for three days to remove residual whey. It is then rewrapped and stored

Each cheese is turned daily for two weeks to check that it is ripening and maturing correctly. For the following three to six months it is turned weekly

The finished Birdoswald handmade cheeses ready to eat

only to sell to people who would continue to farm. Eric and Dianne were granted time to sell their Yorkshire farm, rather than sell off Slack House in parts.

The Horns have been members of the Conservation Society for thirty years, which is an organisation that helps to improve the environment. Dianne has worked as a rural science teacher and they started their conversion to organic farming in the late 1990s. "We had to decide whether to get bigger or to find a niche market." says Eric, "We can't say we make pots of money but conventional farmers have to look at green issues these days too and it's always something we've leaned towards, so it seemed the obvious way to go. Certification by the Soil Association means that we are with an association whose standards and ethos reflect our own."

I had previously tasted Birdoswald cheese, which is a smooth hard Cheddar like cheese with quite a strong, nutty flavour, and was keen to see exactly how it was made.

Eric milks his thirty Ayrshire milking cows at 6.30 each morning and the milk is then pumped straight into the dairy. This milk is unpasteurised in keeping with traditional cheese-making methods which Eric first learnt at agricultural college in Cheshire. When he attended a cheese-making course in Exeter, he was introduced to a 1688 recipe for Ayrshire sweet-milk cheese. After taking over Slack House Farm, Eric's cheese-making knowledge came to the fore, and with old recipes in mind

he started to experiment. Ayrshire milk has a high butterfat content making it ideal for cheese-making.

Thornby Moor Dairy, near Wigton, who use Shorthorn Dairy milk for their farmhouse cheeses gave support and encouragement to help Eric set up Birdoswald Cheese. Thornby Moor also makes a 'cheddar' type cheese which has a different bite to it, being made from a different milk. I believe that Thornby Moor produce the best smoked cheese I've tasted in Britain and with more than twenty-five years cheese-making experience, they were best qualified to help Birdoswald. Both dairies are members of the Specialist Cheesemakers Association, and are the only two farmhouse cheese-makers in the county to my knowledge.

Commercial cheese takes milk from numerous intensively farmed dairies over a large area with milk from many different breeds of cow. It is wrapped in plastic and matured in plastic. The resulting cheese is uniform and bland. In France they pride themselves on regional cheeses, as we should in Britain. Eric believes that cheese-making is influenced by the soil, climate and even the mood of the cheese-maker. "I can use the same recipe over again", he says, "but no two cheeses taste the same." And so Eric was determined to make a cheese specific to his herd, his farm and his expertise.

Unpasteurised milk is held in a forty gallon vat at body temperature before a freeze-dried starter culture is introduced. It is left to ripen for one hour to encourage lactic acid-producing bacteria to grow. A vegetarian rennet is added which helps the milk set. Most hard cheeses contain rennet which is an ingredient taken from the stomach of unweaned calves; vegetarian rennet however is sourced from plants or fungi. The next step is to cut the curd both horizontally and vertically. The resulting cubes of curd are kept in suspension until they shrink; this may take one and a half hours of stirring. "I keep feeling it until it gets to the right texture" says Eric whose hands are spotlessly clean and constantly wet from dipping them in a weak hypochlorite solution. The outside temperature also plays a part in the process and as long as the warm temperature is maintained, the curds behave. Eric doesn't like the cold.

The whey is drained off and recycled as a drink for the cows. The curds are now at what Eric calls 'chicken breast texture' and are milled by hand before they are salted and placed in the large warmed moulds that have been lined with cheese cloths. The large cheese press is then put into service and places a weight on the cheeses for three days. By this time the excess liquid will have been removed and each cheese is re-wrapped, this time in muslin before the storage procedure commences. Ideally Eric likes to store his cheese for at least three months and preferably for six. The dry surroundings of the storeroom are necessary for the cheese to ripen and go hard. Each cheese is turned every day by hand and checked for temperature and humidity, to prevent drying out and to keep conditions constant. If the temperature rises too much the cheese may dry, crack and mature too rapidly, spoiling the texture and the taste.

Eric sells his Birdoswald cheese from the farm gate, by mail order as well as on stalls at local farmers' markets through membership of Hadrian Organics which acts as a marketing co-operative.

Organic farming and membership of the Soil Association has led to involvement with the Countryside Stewardship scheme. This has brought help with restoring dry-stone walls on the farm, relaying hedges, revitalising ponds and planting trees. "We've seen a wonderful return in the wild life here" said Eric who has spotted voles, night jars, buzzards, kestrels, sparrow hawks and three different species of owl. "We have this thriving environment at Slack House, and we like to connect the public with our agriculture." With this in mind as part of an educational aspect to their work, Dianne and Eric are converting another small barn to enable people to see each stage in the process of cheese-making.

You can see the pride and satisfaction on Eric's face when he holds one of his Birdoswalds. Craft cheese production made on such a small scale requires a considerable investment of time and effort, but has qualities far surpassing mass-produced blocks.

"I make two twenty-pound cheeses a week and I don't intend to increase the range of my cheeses at present, I just want to get this one right." Judging from his smile I would think that Eric is enjoying doing just that.

Fresh double cream arrives daily at the farm to begin the butter making process

I have used Cream of Cumbria butter throughout my recipes as an essential ingredient for flavour. Although pastry is often easier to make using lard or half the quantity of lard and half of butter (as my Mum does) I find the flavour of butter hard to beat.

Cream Of Cumbria Butter

Sue and Tom Forrester have been dairy farmers in the low lying plain that divides England from Scotland all their married life. Both are from farming families and grew up milking cows. In 2000 Sue attended a Farming Women's conference in Keswick where I was doing a cookery demonstration. As I cooked for the 200 or so women I bemoaned the fact that Cumbria is a dairy county and we have gallons of milk, but no one making butter – why not? Sue Forrester was one of those Farming Women; she went home that night and told Tom "we're going to make butter!"

Sue started in her kitchen selling butter to family and friends who agreed the butter was like nothing else they could buy. As the year went on Sue realised that she would have to continue making butter as the farm was over its milk quota and they didn't want to be fined for over-production. The only other alternative use of excess milk was to feed it to calves. Sue skimmed off the cream and started making butter in earnest. The red tape attached to this sort of business was, amazingly, surmountable and Cream of Cumbria was born. Sue went along to her first farmers' market in 2000 with forty half pound blocks of butter, twenty packets of buttermilk scones and in twenty minutes she could have gone home - she had sold out.

on the weather

It is essential to rinse under running water to ensure all the buttermilk is removed, to prevent it from souring. Salt is added at this stage

The cream thickens gradually and the colour deepens

Scotch Hands are used to shape each weighed block. Sue uses her grandmothers' "marks" to denote salted and unsalted finished blocks of freshly churned Cumbrian butter

As cream separates into butter and buttermilk, the mass is scraped down and the buttermilk is seived off

Cream of Cumbria Butter

Sue tempts Annette, as if she needs tempting!

As with many others in Cumbria, the outbreak of Foot and Mouth Disease in 2001 changed their lives. The restrictions set to control the disease meant that people as well as animals couldn't leave their farms. Sue maintains however that although they were surrounded by the disease, putting aloe vera in the animals' drinking water kept the disease away from their herd. As farms around them fell to FMD Sue and Tom sat tight and thought about the future. When life got easier they decided to concentrate on butter-making as the core of their business. Other farmers nearby who had lost their herds completely and who wanted to restock contacted Sue and Tom, so they had buyers for their Holstein Friesian dairy herd.

Making butter by hand is an intensive, lengthy process that is often affected by temperature and weather conditions. Sue usually makes butter two or three days a week in a converted extension to her farmhouse kitchen with her good friend Carol Graham completing the butter-making team. Old fashioned churns, lined with a plastic inner, are delivered full of cream each morning to the farm and are kept chilled until needed. Eleven jug-fulls of thick, fresh cream are poured into the large mixer and the churning begins. Whisking continues gently for 30 to 45 minutes depending on the weather until the cream thickens. Carol uses her thick-handled black scraper to push the whipped cream back down into the bowl and eventually the cream turns a darker yellow and coagulates into a substance that resembles scrambled egg. The cream separates out into butterfat and buttermilk. After the machine is switched off, the mass is scraped off the whisk and out of the bowl into a sieve for washing. The butter is sticky at this stage indicating that lactic acid is present. Lactic acid can turn butter rancid and so the thick yellow fat needs to be washed under running water, until the point when the water runs clear. The buttermilk is sieved into containers used in baking and for specific orders. Salt is added if necessary at this point and the butter is then carefully weighed out into 258g lumps. The extra 8 grams is to account for the small residue of liquid that lingers within, which needs to be battered out of the butter during patting. Sue uses the old fashioned wooden butter pats, often called 'scotch hands' to make the blocks. There's a West Cumbrian expression, they say 'give it belfagan'. The origin of this is rather obscure but it remains a common expression. Sue gives it belfagan as she pats the butter, the sound created is enough to make me want to dance! The rhythmical battering to form the rectangles clatters against the work surface as the butter is battered and pressed into shape. When she's quite happy with the result Sue gives the top surface one last press and then marks the top with her distinctive pattern before wrapping and labelling.

"My Mum was there the first day I made butter" Sue explained, "and unprompted, patted the first block of butter and adorned it with the mark that her mother had used eighty years ago when she had taken home-made butter to Haltwhistle." Sue then set off for the other side of the family to discover the mark they had printed on top of their butter. An aged Aunty, the sole survivor, sat and thought for a while then remembered the kiss on the top. Cream of Cumbria's unsalted butter is distinguishable by the family lines and her salted butter is adorned with the family kiss. In the days before mass packaging, when people would sell butter at markets, the consumer had to remember their favourite butter's distinguishing marks.

As Sue aims to be left with nothing at the end of each buttermaking line, nothing is wasted so she sets to and bakes a variety of scones and cakes to be sold at markets. The buttermilk is used as an essential, flavoursome ingredient in her scones, fruit loaves and teabreads. Buttermilk doesn't really describe the fat content of this liquid which is minimal. However buttermilk bought in a supermarket is not the same as it is cultured from skimmed milk and has never been near butter. Sue sells some of her real buttermilk which customers believe has a curative effect. It can be drunk or used in cooking.

Sue has revived Grannie's Clipping Cake – a renowned Cumberland recipe using dried fruit, almonds, treacle and rum which she now calls 'Coast to Coast Cake' – the perfect carbohydrate rush when walking. Another is her Buttermilk slice which has no egg to help the 'keeping' quality of the cake and was previously known as 'Wait while next week cake'.

One of the most traditional of dishes in Cumbria which is used to celebrate a christening is Cumberland Rum Butter. The museum in Whitehaven has examples of large bowls on a tall stem especially for rum butter. The story goes that rum is the spirit of life, sugar is the sweetness of life, nutmeg is the spice of life and butter is the richness of life – an apt present for a new baby. Traditionally a mother-to-be made the butter three months before the baby was due, keeping it under her bed until baby arrived when it was offered to visitors on oatmeal biscuits. Sue describes her Cumberland Rum Butter as "selling by the cuddy load!" (a cuddy is a Cumbrian dialect word for a donkey.)

When Sue's asked about the difference between her butter and that bought in supermarkets, she replies that hers is made by hand, comes from a traceable source of milk and has its very own mark.

"Consumers' tastes are changing," says Sue, "I'm now selling far more unsalted butter, which is good as people are probably cooking with it too." I for one can vouch for that!

Vegetables

The latest government policy encourages everyone to eat at least five portions of fruit and vegetables a day. Vitamins and minerals are essential for good health and are found in abundance in a variety of vegetables. It is widely accepted that to gain maximum benefit it is best to eat vegtables fresh.

Watercress, which is native to Britain, has supplied essential iron and Vitamins A and C to our diet for a thousand years. It can be found growing wild in Cumbria, where it thrives on boggy ground, but it is essential to have knowlege of the water's source before eating. It is advisable to eat commercially grown watercress, as wild watercress can harbour undesirable organisms.

Of course it is easy to mistake one plant for another, and finding a large white rooted vegetable growing wild in my garden made me realise how deadly hemlock has been mistaken for parsnip in the past. Hemlock has a similar leaf and root but the stem has purple flecks. One of the earliest vegetables known to have been cultivated was the humble broad bean, followed by parsnip, cabbage, and peas.

Early explorers traded with the New World, and they brought back home to Britain various vegetables that are now common here. Potatoes, tomatoes, aubergines and peppers came from South America and onions and garlic were eaten in Egypt in 3000 B.C.

It was during the eighteenth and nineteenth centuries that vegetables became popular, coinciding with the Enclosures Acts. From 1760 onwards land was enclosed by field hedges and boundaries by local landowners who claimed it for themselves. Three and half thousand Acts of Parliament were passed between 1760 and 1818, which enclosed five million acres of formerly open land.

In 1845 the government eventually allowed field gardens of not more than a quarter of an acre, because so little

Cutting spinach in the garden

land was available, to enable the poor to grow their own vegetables. These are the forerunner of allotments. Carlisle's first allotment was let in 1910. Allotments have had a change of image recently, younger people, women and children as well as men can now be seen tending their allotments and benefiting from the supply of fresh seasonal vegetables in Cumbria.

Wilfred Lawson, a philanthropist who farmed near Aspatria, admired the work of Joseph Mechie (a farmer from Tiptree, Essex). In 1866 Wilfred and his son William advertised the first of a series of Christmas festivals to promote vegetarianism. These festivals were free to all and offered lectures, musical and other cultural events with a 'fruit, grain and vegetable meal at midday.' It would appear that the Lawsons were men 'before their time' as their principles of co-operation developed Aspatria College as well as Aspatria Farmers, which is the oldest surviving agricultural farmers' co-operative in Britain. Mr Lawson would be proud today of Cumbria's boast of local food for local people as he served only British-grown ingredients. On reflection the meal may have been a trifle dull as it was winter and only root crops, beans, oatmeal and apples were on the menu, mostly uncooked. The following year he introduced beef to appease the masses, cooked the vegetables and charged them a nominal amount.

Interestingly, by the third year of festivals at Mechi, the Carlisle newspaper had to advise

Beetroot straight from the ground

Globe artichokes

that over 2,600 tickets had been sold, and by the beginning of December it was sold out.

Around Carlisle there is a scattering of distinctive houses with hipped roofs which were created by the Land Settlement Association in 1934. These smallholdings, each with an acre or so of land, were leased to local people to assist with pig and poultry keeping and market gardening, following a period of high unemployment and the Depression. Today some still continue the market garden tradition.

It has taken me twenty years to realise that six-feet high runner beans will never survive in my kitchen garden. The Solway winds are strong and I maintain that everything comes ready salted. Most vegetables that I grow are dwarf varieties, but we eat well and I can provide

Yellow courgette

Herb fennel in the early morning sun

Jerusalem artichokes, spinach, leeks and parsnips in the winter months followed by spring cabbage, asparagus, rhubarb, broccoli, cauliflower and chard in the spring and the full range of salad leaves, beans and peas, potatoes, beetroot, courgettes, onions and garlic, herbs and soft fruit in the summer; with pumpkins, apples and pears to finish the year. Growing your own really does mean you can eat the freshest and ripest produce with the best flavour at the right time of the year. What more can I say to convince you that it's a worthwhile pastime?

Tim Copsey knows about seasons. His family have farmed a market garden at Camerton, near Workington, for five generations and the business is famous locally for winter crops. Tim has glasshouses and polytunnels on the south-facing slope of his land and is able to sell tomatoes and

Tim Copsey with his International tractor

Tim Copsey checks his leeks for taste

lettuce in the summer, but he also has fields of glaucous blue leeks and potatoes amongst his 110 acres. "I was in the post office the other day and the woman behind me asked if I could smell onions. I had to laugh, I'd been picking leeks all morning!"

Tim still tends his land using an ancient International tractor which superseded Dolly, the shire horse, twenty years ago. (He won't be getting the same fertiliser from the tractor that he got from Dolly!)

Tim supplies twenty food co-ops in Workington, Whitehaven and Carlisle, plus five in Maryport. These co-ops are based in community centres and schools, and enable people to buy fresh, seasonal vegetables at a fair price.

Typically, members of the co-operative can buy a £2 vegetable bag, which could contain two kilos of potatoes, one kilo of carrots, one cauliflower, one turnip/swede and two broccoli heads. The rest of his crops are sold on to wholesalers who supply local hotels. Tim says that there are only two months of the year when he's not actually cutting crops, in which case he's planting for the following season.

He's quite philosophical about his life. "People aren't prepared to pay for food anymore," he says, "they just want cheap food, and it's a vicious circle as they buy from supermarkets who screw down the price of the vegetables from us. Things have got to change. I'm not surprised or saddened that none of my children are interested in carrying on W. Copsey and Sons. I love the outdoor life but they'll have an easier work load doing something else."

Rose Wolfe plants tomato seeds

Rose's Green Grape tomatoes

Rose Wolfe knows about work, too. She has two large glasshouses next to her home in Allerby in West Cumbria and raises an amazing quantity of tomatoes, peppers, chillies, cucumber and herbs. Rose is particularly interested in tomatoes with flavour and searches for old varieties which she starts off in March each year. Inside one of her glasshouses she has a bubble-wrapped inner house, which enables an early start for her seedlings. "I still can't get them going out into the main glass house until the sun really warms up," Rose says, "but once they're off there's no stopping them". The hands of tomato fruits are lengthy and there's a warm musky scent of ripening tomatoes as she walks along the upright cordons in summer. One of my favourite tomatoes that Rose grows each year is Green Grape, a heritage variety over one hundred years old, which has a deceptive sweetness though it is mottled green and pale yellow. She has many yellow and orange varieties too as well as plum tomatoes, which are not juicy but have plenty of flesh to make classic Mediterranean-style sauces. As Rose is successful in her initial sowing of seeds, she sells her seedlings at local market stalls in the spring for others to grow.

At the other end of the county amongst woodland and limestone outcrops lies Howbarrow Organic

Farm which Paul Hughes and Julia Sayburn established in 1996.

This is a permanent pasture hill farm, specific to Cumbria with very little top soil, probably only nine inches. Primarily they produce an extensive range of horticultural, culinary and medicinal herbs, vegetables in season as well as beef, sheep and Christmas poultry.

Both Paul and Julia were qualified to teach but their previous lives didn't entirely equip them for their life today. Julia had lived in southern Ireland where she had a house cow, and Paul had run a double allotment with a pig. Both had gardened organically however. Once they realised that they were having trouble conceiving a baby, they looked at their diet and were concerned about the impact of conventional food on male fertility. They decided to grow more organic food, eat more organic food and drink organic wine. They now have two lovely daughters, though are quick to say that they can't claim that their lifestyle was the answer.

Julia Sayburn and Paul Hughes

A pest controller working in the polytunnel

Part of their organic growing encompasses the building up of fertility in the soil. They do this by planting in rotation, both with the animals and fields as well as in the garden and polytunnels. They plant green manure such as clovers, peas and beans which fix nitrogen in the soil. They use animal manure, though they can't produce enough on the farm as their animals are not housed. They also make a comfrey liquid from huge beds of comfrey which line the outside of the polytunnels, and they make compost which is returned to the soil.

Small dedicated houses for butterflies, lacewings and ladybirds can be seen around the farm which they have erected to help the insects over-winter and breed. These then act as pest control agents during the growing season. A discreet pond is situated close to the polytunnels

Chives just coming into season

My girls help with the digging!

as a frog hatchery; the frogs devour greenfly, slugs and snails, and it's not unusual to see them hopping about the polytunnels doing their duty. By growing a diverse number of plants in any one area they aim to attract the predators; honeysuckle and a vine sit comfortably with courgettes and climbing beans in the tunnel.

Paul says, "No one thing helps to keep an ecological balance, it's a range of things combined. As small producers we prefer a natural growth rate in our vegetables, it's better for the plants' structure and better for flavour. We've taken on a derelict farm and turned it into a thriving business.

Everything has been learnt by mistakes over time. After FMD lots of farms have had to look at direct selling; it's the way forward for us, our holding is highly productive. At first the local farmers thought us wacky going into direct selling, and apparently good money changed hands on how long we'd last! Well, we now have an NVQ in roller coasting and an overdraft project, but we're all healthy and happy."

Pork

There is a saying that you can eat everything on a pig except the squeak! And anyone that has held a new piglet will know just how much noise they make.

In days gone by when people were dependent on pigs' meat for their families, they made the most of each animal, and consequently there are recipes for using every part. Most villages would have had at least two pork processors making ham, bacon as well as haslet and brawn for local consumption.

Bar Woodall's family have been curing and selling pork products since 1828 in the small

> ROYAL AGRICULTURAL SOCIETY'S
> INTERNATIONAL SHOW, KILBURN,
> June 30 to July 7, 1879.
>
> **SECOND PRIZE**
> AWARDED TO
> **RICHARD WOODALL, Bacon Curer,**
> WABERTHWAITE, VIA CARNFORTH,
> CUMBERLAND,
> FOR
> **SIX BRITISH HAMS.**

West Cumbrian village of Waberthwaite, where he remembers rubbing salt into pork sides as a tiny boy. Bar is proud of the family's 1879 second prize certificate for six British dry cured hams received in London at the International Dairy Show. As he

Bar Woodall in the shop at Waberthwaite

Cumbrian dry cured bacon

says, "It was a heck of an achievement in those days as so many people were competing. Then the animal was kept for over two years before it was considered fit for eating, which today would appear as a pensionable age for a pig. It was given the equivalent of four pounds of food to produce one pound of finished pork – today they are given under two pounds of food to produce the same weight. And there's been a big change in the shape of the pig too, the carcass is becoming leaner."

The Woodall family are very proud of the fact that in 1999 they were awarded the royal warrant to supply Buckingham Palace with bacon and ham. "It's been a wonderful recognition of the quality of our business," says Bar. He and his wife June are intent on preserving the royal loyalty and make a point of going to pay a courtesy call every year.

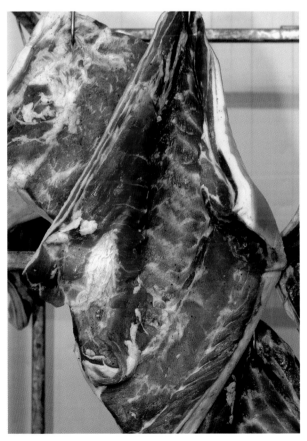

Sides of bacon

During the middle of the 19th century Danish bacon producers purposely bred a very productive pig known as the Landrace. After the Second World War, Britain started to import huge amounts of bacon from Denmark and our traditional breeds were pushed aside.

Cumberland had its own pig. It was a much-prized beast with large jowls, floppy ears that covered its eyes, an upturned snout (said to be dished) and a high fat content that made good hams. It was heavy-boned, slow to mature and extremely hardy. Just the sort of animal that suited living in the Cumberland climate. It gave its name to recipes and pork produce that link our old county name – Cumberland Ham and Cumberland Sausage. Sadly, the Cumberland pig was allowed to die out in the 1960s.

Savin Hill Farm in the Lythe Valley, south Cumbria, produces Middle White pigs which are said to be the nearest thing to the original Cumberland Pig today.

Peter Gott of Sillfield Farm is attempting to reintroduce this long lost pig. He started a few years back breeding from a Middle White boar from Kirkham prison in Lancashire (prison farms have now given up keeping pigs which seems a shame), and is continuing to cross them with pure Lops. As part of his research he visited the Loweswater Show and says, "I met an auld fella who reckoned that he remembered the Cumberland pig and said that to identify one you had to give the pig a good smack, then look at its skin, your hand would have left an imprint in the flesh." Peter says that it may be a year or two before his version

of the Cumberland Pig is born and until then Tamworths, Saddlebacks, Gloucester Old Spots and Middle Whites are thriving in Cumbria.

For hundreds of years pork has been cured with salt to produce bacon and ham. In fact, salt has been used to preserve food for thousands of years and was especially important before refrigeration. The cures for ham were as various as the areas from which they came. One book from the early 1800s describes using horse litter for a stronger flavour! When most homes would have had their own pig, it would have been fed on scraps and allowed to scavenge for wild food and

Peter Gott of Sillfield Farm

Jon Perkin with Mango hie Tamworth sow and piglets

the resulting meat would have been salted and smoked to keep the family going over the leaner winter months. When I see the rows of hooks hanging in our pantry and inside the fire hood I can imagine the smoky flavour of big fat hams from the family pig, but that was before the days of environmental health! We may think that air-dried ham is an Italian invention but in Cumbria we've probably been air drying just as long.

Essentially bacon is made by curing pork, hanging, maturing, possibly smoking and then slicing. Traditionally bacon can be either dry or wet cured. To dry cure bacon, sides of pork are rubbed by hand with salt and spices pushing the mixture into every crevice; the sides are stacked, packed in this salt mixture for a couple of weeks. In the wet-curing process the pork is soaked in a liquid curing solution. After curing the bacon is washed, dried and left to mature for a couple of weeks. Depending on the producer, the complete process may take as long as six weeks.

Large scale, industrial bacon production is a much quicker process. Curing may take only a day, with the use of a strong salt solution. Often it is pre-sliced to further speed the process. The brine solution that is used removes naturally-occurring moisture, so liquid is injected back into the bacon, this liquid produces the objectionable white gunge that leaks from packed bacon when it is cooked.

Over the last twenty or thirty years these practices have allowed a twenty pound piece of pork to become a twenty one pound piece of ham. In the old days using the lengthier process a twenty pound piece of pork became a fifteen pound ham.

Tamworth piglets

Whiteholme Farm lies up in the hills among slightly undulating and boggy countryside. Even when there's only been a little rain it looks damp. The tussock grass poking up in the scrubby fields is a give-away of the moisture it so loves. Jon and Lynne Perkin have been farming here for more than three years and they seem to have acclimatised well from their Cornish origins.

The Hadrian Organics brochure describes their farm as an 85 hectare grassland farm, but forget lush green rolling hills, this is a harsh climate. However, the good husbandry of Jon and Lynne means that they succeed in conditions where others might not. They produce traditional pure breeds of pork, beef and lamb. Their Tamworth boar has to work hard. Each sow has two litters

per year and as the gestation period for the pig is three months, three weeks and three days, their calculations need clever timing to achieve this. Most sows will give birth to eight to ten piglets in one litter.

The Tamworth pig is a hardy creature that grows slowly and produces a well-flavoured meat.

Because winters are cold and damp in north Cumbria all the pigs are kept inside with access to the slippery mud outside. They are dependent on heat to grow so during the winter months it takes longer for them to fatten. They are fed on a high protein diet that is mostly maize (with the addition of barley, bran and peas) until they are about four and a half months old. When they are six months old they travel the short distance to the small, organic abattoir in Lockerbie. Some piglets were sold on for breeding, but as Jon and Lynne aspire to being able to trace their meat products from start to finish and the demand for their meat has increased, they now can't grow enough to keep up with it. As Jon says "the bacon is just flying out the door"!

At Whiteholme Farm they cure their bacon in small pieces. The sides of the pork make back bacon, the flanks make streaky, and the shoulders make collar bacon. Lynne and Jon have a converted byre made into a state-of-the-art butchery where they work. Both Tamworth and Saddleback pigs make good bacon as they have a fair content of fat. The pieces of meat are boned and rubbed with the dry-cure mix of salt, salt petre (potassium nitrate) plus an ingredient that is secret to Whiteholme. The bacon is left for a week in this dry cure; ham is given two weeks. After the salt has drawn out the water from the meat, they wash away the residue cure, hang it up to dry for a day or so and then put it in the freezer for two to three hours before slicing. Lynne has previously worked in a bacon factory where all the bacon sides used to come in deep chilled and she felt this was one technique that they could copy. Slicing is easier when the meat is cold. "I personally prefer decent sized rashers, it makes the bacon more of a meal, so I tend to slice four to five millimetre slices," says Lynne. Having tried both wet and dry cures with their home grown porkers Lynne and Jon have found that the dry method was preferred by their customers.

Beef

Roast beef is arguably Britain's national dish. The French have given us the nick name 'Les rosbifs' and many people around the world associate British cookery with our traditional Sunday meal.

In medieval times a farmer who couldn't afford to feed his beasts during the long winter months often preserved meat by salting to keep it palatable. However the cost of salt and spices required to preserve using this method meant that only the best quality meat was salted; this probably originated the saying that tough or stringy meat just 'wasn't worth the salt'. Beef was boiled, served with lots of root vegetables and seasoned again before being served 'swimming in butter'. There is a Salted Beef recipe in the section at the back of this book that doesn't have to be served with the butter, as salting produces great succulence. Salt petre was traditionally used which gives a pink colour, though it's difficult to source these days unless you know an interested pharmacist! Plain salt works just as well.

Roast beef is fairly straightforward to cook, however the following few points can greatly improve the quality of the joint. It is best to take it out of the fridge for at least an hour before placing into a preheated oven. Once fully cooked, remove from the oven, keeping it warm and draught free for twenty minutes to 'rest' before carving. This resting time provides the opportunity to make gravy from the residue from the roasting tin and helps keep the moisture in the meat.

Borrowdale the bull with one of his Longhorn cows

Susan Aglionby with one of her Longhorn cows

Longhorn Cattle

Susan Aglionby declares that her life is dominated by sex. She started work as a family planning nurse in 1970 and has been a Longhorn beef farmer since 1990. She's constantly wondering if the bull is doing his job or if the calving heifer is expecting twins or triplets and she's keen to make sure that 'every child is a wanted child'. Susan believes that nursing is a great background for anyone who wishes to enter farming: "I've worked mostly in neurosurgery where everyone was unconscious, so working with animals who can't tell you what's wrong is just another extension of that."

The Longhorn is an ancient breed of cattle that appealed to Susan when she first decided to become a farmer, as its origins are northern. They have distinctive colouring; mottled dark plum to light roan with white patches on the legs and 'flinching' down their backs.

The breed dates back to the 18th century, when Robert Bakewell of Leicestershire took a Longhorn bull (called Twopenny) from Westmorland and began the development of the beef breed that we know today. Originally their milk was valued for butter making but Robert Bakewell's only interest was in an animal for meat with an early-maturing carcass and a high proportion of fat. In the mid 1800s the majority of beef cattle in the Midlands were this improved Longhorn type, but the glory was short-lived and only enthusiasts kept the breed going until today when these fine looking beasts have become popular once again for their quality meat. They are hardy, live outside all the year round and do well on poor land. In fact Susan's water meadow with its rushes can be considered an ideal pasture for Borrowdale the bull and his 'wives'.

This breed calve easily and their long horns belie their docile nature. The calves stay with their mothers to suckle for at least seven months and the beasts are aged about thirty months when they are slaughtered. The meat is hung from between two and three weeks to improve the flavour and finished texture. Interestingly, many other Longhorn breeders are women.

Susan has just over a hundred acres, which includes a woodland - the first community wood in Cumbria planted in 1993 with mostly oak trees where she keeps sheep in the springtime. Unfortunately her farmland is split into two areas fourteen miles apart. "It's totally mad I know, and I wouldn't be able to work as I do if it wasn't for the help of family and friends. I do believe that Trim the sheepdog (who was bought ready trained from a shepherd in Threlkeld) will enable me to go on farming for years longer."

It is hard to imagine from these photographs that Susan farms not two miles from Carlisle city centre and she has her bus pass. Croft Farm is part of Hadrian Organics marketing co-operative which was formed in 2003. Susan sells directly from the farm and having established the quality of her meat, she now has a waiting list for the beef.

Susan is quite philosophical about life and farming:"We have the responsibility to pass our land onto our children in good fettle." After the foot and mouth outbreak of 2001 when Susan saw all her stock destroyed, she decided that the only way forward was to become organic and in 2005 she saw the first of her organic herd through from calving to slaughter.

"Cleaning up, finding new stock and then breeding from them has taken time, however it is wonderful to see pedigree Longhorn cattle in the fields and to have so many customers to buy my meat."

Susan Aglionby in the water meadow

Herdwick Sheep

Cumbrian mythology suggests that Herdwick sheep came over from Scandinavia with the Vikings. They have survived on the roughest pastures on the Lakeland fell tops since then, evolving into the breed we see today. It is thought that the Lake District looks as it does because of the Herdwicks. They garden the Lake District fells, keeping the area well cropped. No one applies fertiliser on the open fell, it is a completely natural environment and Herdwick share their food with wild deer.

One characteristic of Herdwick is their shortness of leg, being rather stocky. Other features are a white face that looks as if it's smiling and a coarse fleece.

Joe Relph and Annette herd the sheep

They produce very hard-wearing and coarse wool containing lots of kemp. This is the rough guard hair under which they have a layer of fine wool that keeps them warm. The kemp weatherproofs the sheep, shedding rainwater. There are stories of Herdwick having survived snowstorms for weeks at 3000 feet owing to their waterproof wool. These insulating qualities are exploited today by use in house insulating material as well as in the clothing industry. Herdwick wool has not traditionally been used for knitting as it is 'itchy' owing to its coarse nature. However it is now sold at country fairs and a small number of enthusiasts knit garments with Herdwick wool.

The old fashioned method of fell farming before the war meant that Herdwick sheep would have been killed at four or five years old having grown slowly on the fells. These Herdwick were naturally fat and the farmer could have benefited from four or five crops of wool, at a time when wool was valuable. Mutton was popular with consumers before the war.

The Hill Farming Act was introduced after the war, giving subsidies to farmers to encourage increased production. Times have changed and so have tastes, and today quick cooking techniques have superseded recipes that recommended long, slow cooking. Lamb is now preferred over mutton.

Herdwick farming has changed too, and although the systems are similar, the end product is adapted to present day palates.

Each animal grows slowly and Herwicks have large bones to help cope with the rough terrain. Their diet consists of wild herbs, juniper, heathers and low growing grasses which thrive on the fellside. What little fat they do produce has been likened to olive oil with high omega 3 fatty acid content. This is possibly due to them having been fed on grass for a lengthy period. Interestingly, omega 3 is otherwise found in fish, but as Herdwicks are probably in as much water as the fish it's no great surprise! Rainfall on the fell tops can exceed a hundred inches a year.

The resulting meat has a depth of flavour that some say reminds them of how meat used to taste.

The Herdwicks lamb later than other sheep, as is usual with hill breeds. The ewes typically have their first lambs at three years old when most other breeds would have had at least one lamb. Herdwick lambs are born with nearly black fleece and white ears in April and May each year. One way to recognise Herdwick is that the older they get the greyer they become, rather like people, and grey-white fleeced mothers run with chocolate brown year-old babies.

Herdwick wool has been used in carpet manufacture for many years. The natural changes of coloration of the different aged animals have been used to great effect to create attractive carpets that resemble tweed.

Take one look at Joe Relph and you can see that he belongs in the Borrowdale valley. He appears to tower up like the surrounding fells, he's six feet six inches tall, and just like the fells, he stands proud with his boots firmly fixed in the earth. He has a deep love for the countryside and its inhabitants.

Joe and his wife Hazel have farmed in Borrowdale since the 1980s; this is but a short time compared to the years that Herdwicks have been bred in the valley. In the high fells of the English Lake District, Herdwick sheep have lived for a thousand years. Each Herdwick has special knowledge that means that it knows where it lives and stays local to its area. Each animal passes this information down from generation to generation creating a close connection between Cumbria's own sheep and the landscape itself; free-grazing sheep help keep the fells open for all to enjoy. This characteristic is known as 'heafing' or 'hefting' and it was thought that after Foot and Mouth Disease hit the county in 2001, that their innate knowledge might be lost. Between a third to a half of the breed was culled and breeders are rebuilding their flocks and continuing the age-old task of trying to make a living from fell farms.

Joe and Hazel, with their son Stephen, farm 2000 sheep over 2000 acres.

Hazel says, "The thing that pleases us the most, is the guaranteed traceability of our meat. They're born here, they grow here, they fatten here, they're a day away to the abattoir, hung and butchered here, vac packed here, cooked here, and put into a hamper here. We had an opportunity to send our meat to London, but no, that's the whole point of regional food,

Herdwick sheep

people must come here to eat it, in its own surroundings.

And what makes a traditionally made product? In our case there's nothing to do to change it. Simple. Herdwicks have always grown slowly.

A lowland lamb that's been fed on improved pasture is ready to kill between three and six months old; they may be tender, but they'll have no flavour. Our Herdwick will be between ten and eighteen months when they go; it's seasonal meat too, they get to the right weight individually.

The ewes come into the lower fields to lamb, and as soon as it's on its feet it'll go to the "intake", [a protected fenced area lower on the fellside] they'll still be with their mothers and then they're weaned at about four months. We keep them in open barns inside during the winter for the seriously cold months when they're about seven months old. They have their own silage, chopped very small so that it's easy for the lambs to eat. Plus a ready made feed, mostly barley. They could be outside but it's so cold and wet here, we consider it good husbandry to look after them. And then it's up onto the open fell where mum takes it to the hefting part. We bring them in to clip them. Just the mums get dosed, injected, dipped and then straight back on to the fell.

At birth we decide which males we'll keep for breeding as a tup. The rest will be kept for eating, and all females are kept for breeding. We've got to keep young sheep at the fell as the old ones die off."

When buying Herdwick, Hazel offers recommendations on cooking. She says that at between ten months and fourteen months Herdwick cooks like lamb, each cut tender as fillet, so quick roasting and flash frying is fine. After fourteen months to eighteen months it cooks differently, tastes as good but needs a little more time and this is when Tatie Pot or slow cooked casseroles are more suitable dishes.

Some original Herdwick recipes were made at Christmas using fruity combinations of apples and Herdwick in minced meat dishes. Damsons, too, compliment the meat and the Relphs add apricots to their Herdwick sausages.

Sheep farming in Cumbria has developed a language of its own. The animal starts life as a lamb, when it is weaned it becomes a hog. After it has been shorn for the first time at around eighteen months it is a shearling, or twinter (it has had its second winter), when it has been shorn twice it is called a two shear, then three shear and so on.

Wethers are castrated males; this happens when they are only one week old. Breeding males are called tups or tips. Gimmer lamb is a young female, which becomes a gimmer hog, then a gimmer shearling and finally a ewe, often pronounced yow.

It is fondly believed that shepherds when counting their flock avoid the conventional one, two three. Different valleys have different spelling and pronunciation. These sheep scoring numerals – a traditional dialect way of counting sheep – go yan, tyan, tethera, methera, pimp, sethera, lethera, hovera, dovera, dick. It continues yan a dick, tyan a dick progressively.

Venison

Originally the word venison applied to any furred game but now the term is generally used to describe the meat of deer. Deer are the most recent animals to be domesticated although many are still wild animals. Modern consumers don't always appreciate the strong 'gamey' flavour found in wild venison. In Cumbria it is still a privilege to come across deer running wild and if you become familiar with the countryside, it is possible to discover their shelter-belts and grazing ground. During the quiet time of spring 2001 when movement of farm animals was restricted due to Foot and Mouth Disease, deer were seen wandering down to the beach on Cumbria's west coast.

Wild deer has to be hung to induce tenderness and by doing so the meat can become dry.

Traditionally wild venison was rubbed with powdered ginger and pepper when hung, to prevent it from 'going off'. This may have repelled flying insects too, though this obviously didn't always work as old recipe books would give instructions on how to rescue tainted venison.

Lakeland recipe books recommend roasting haunches of venison and serving it with red cabbage, but never with a green vegetable. Potting was popular, as a means of preserving, by cooking the meat and covering it with clarified butter.

Wild venison has a stronger, gamey taste than farmed venison and consequently is often marinaded to compensate for the lack of moisture.

Marinading venison, usually in red wine or port to make the meat moist is questionable as alcohol draws moisture from the meat. Marinading in oil and spices would help. Traditionally larding of venison was done using a larding needle to incorporate slivers of fat, usually pork or bacon, into a roast, today this process is done by slitting the meat and studding it with the fat.

Farmed venison however is flavoursome, tender and doesn't tend to be dry, though it has little actual fat.

A red stag

Peter Stoeken and Jane Emerson

Jane Emerson and Peter Stoeken farm five hundred red deer with eight stags on their farm at Penruddock, near Penrith. It is a delightful setting for them all.

The farm is obtaining organic accreditation from the Soil Association. To achieve organic conversion the animals have to be conceived on the farm. In the summer of 2006 they will be fully organic.

Jane and Peter have been farming deer for almost twenty years and on reflection they say that "If it can go wrong, it will go wrong it has gone wrong!"

Previously they kept a range of deer species; Red Fallow with Sika, Pere Davide and Wapiti from Canada. These were all slaughtered because of Foot and Mouth Disease in 2001.

Jane, Peter and Annette with friends

They restocked the farm in mid 2002 with Red Deer only, deciding to keep life simple. If only they knew what was going to happen. It took a long time to clean up and get ready and on advice they bought in Cumbrian deer which, unbeknown to them, all had TB! The complete herd had to be killed.

Peter and Jane now both have a wonderful black sense of humour.

They didn't restock till May 2003 and continue to farm Red Deer.

Jane and Peter are not control freaks (their own words), but believe that deer need to be handled. "One day they may be in to be ear tagged, one day they're butchered. We want

to keep their stress levels down so we control the quality of the deer from birth to your plate – then it's your fault if you've cooked it badly!" says Peter.

Jane describes them as ". . . fed on herb rich grass in wild flower meadows. It's called permanent pasture which we manage through grazing and cutting and which we can improve by adding plants. We never take off hay. The deer don't undergraze, nor overgraze, we're always moving them around the farm and the stocking levels are such that they are in balance with the amount of grazing.

The high clover swards are rich in nitrogen which we sow. We grow turnips for the deer to eat in situ which they pass through their bodies as fertiliser at the other end.

Our aim is to produce all our own food. But we can't grow grain, it's just not warm enough here and it's too steep, though we're thinking of growing oats. We've done some mixed grains and made it into silage at the green stage. When the grain goes milky the cereal head is turned into silage and we cut it, wilt it and chop it, then it's baled as opposed to clamping as silage. Most years growing silage, we get two cuts and possibly three if the growth and weather conditions are right."

Deer breed outside from October to November; it is possible to hear them roaring during rutting and the whole valley can hear them. A single stag is in with one group of up to forty five hinds at a time. Their antlers are cut off in the rutting season to prevent any problems as the males start to assert themselves. Antlers grow annually and are the fastest growing animal tissue of all. They can protrude to nearly a metre high.

Size determines fertility, in the wild, deer usually weigh about 70kg when mature enough to breed. At Old Stoddah Farm deer are always about two years old and have reached 90kg before going to the stag. Animals that fail to reach this weight have to take the other route - to the abattoir instead.

"We're living in a very wet part of Cumbria. We try to leave the animals out till Christmas. Silage is fed to our animals during winter when they are housed inside in open barns.

Fawn are born in June each year. Depending on weather conditions and if we have enough grass, we leave the babies with the hinds until they are four months old which keeps the hinds in good condition. They can calve for twenty years and they tend to calve easily, with only one in a thousand requiring an assisted birth. It is necessary to inspect the stock twice a day; our systems enable us to watch out for trouble and bring them in quickly." Jane and Peter are with their deer as much as possible to get the animals used to them and the necessary farming routines. "They're with us for a long time and become like old friends. I don't like killing my beasts. The trauma of killing 408 to Foot and Mouth and approximately 200 to TB has put me off. We do enjoy breeding the animals but I question what I do and it's the one thing that could turn me into being a veggie. My conscience bothers me that I have to kill," says Peter.

Deer at Old Stoddah Farm are ready for eating between 14 and 24 months and are slaughtered at the purpose-built premises on the farm. It is necessary to have a vet in attendance at the death of each animal and there are regular inspections from the Meat Hygiene Service.

It felt like a privilege to be there in the field with Peter and Jane surrounded by a handful of curious stags. In early summer, they are shy and curious, not threatening at all; their hormones haven't kicked in. And don't they look grand.

Sausage

You can tell a Cumberland Sausage by its shape, which is laid in a continuous spiral. Traditionally made from pork, it is chunky, coarse cut and spiced with pepper, and is often sold by length.

Sausages have been made for thousands of years throughout the world and have been a local speciality in Cumbria for around five hundred years. There is debate about the creation of Cumberland sausages, one theory being that German miners who came to Cumbria in Queen Elizabeth I's reign brought with them a thick meaty sausage to sustain them; another explanation is that the coiled loops provided a practical means of combining a selection of ingredients in a single skin. However the history is anecdotal; nothing has been recorded, but it is irrefutable that the Cumberland Sausage that can be seen proudly displayed around the county's butchers' shops has a culinary heritage

Producers of genuine Cumberland Sausage make it to a high standard with at least 95 per cent and often more meat content. Mass-produced look-a-likes sacrificed quality by using emulsified pork, filling with rusk in thinner spirals. This devaluation of the product has led to action now being taken to protect Cumberland sausage through European legislation. It is planned for the sausage to be granted a PGI (Product Geographical Indication) along with Parma ham, Normandy cheeses, Scotch beef, and Jersey Royal potatoes, so that only sausages with specified meat, spice content, processing and place of origin could be called Cumberland. Peter Gott of Sillfield Farm, near Kendal has been instrumental in achieving this certification.

Richard Woodall (known as Bar after his mother's maiden name) of Waberthwaite and his family have been producing sausage, ham and bacon for nearly two hundred years. In 1939 a government representative of the then Ministry of Food, visited Waberthwaite and directed that the proportions of rusk and water in their Cumberland Sausage were to be increased as the war developed, in order that the rations should go further. Bar remembers his father being quite perturbed and saying that as this step would compromise the reputation of his sausage he would prefer to stop making them. Not knowing

Bar and June Woodall

Traditional Cumbrian Sausage

how long the war would last, it took five years before production started again. The Woodall stock is a closed herd of mainly Landrace pigs with Large White females. They tend to have 180 breeding sows and 2000 pigs at any one time.

"We don't buy any breeding stock, we use A.I. [artificial insemination] and our pigs enjoy a high health status, with no hormone growth promoters; and although the feed used to be fish meal it's now only vegetable protein, ground nut cake and vegetable based protein," Bar says with pride.

Bar remembers that by the 1960s a traditional Cumberland sausage was hard to find.

This is hardly surprising when one considers the advent of processed cheap food which was encouraged after the war when the Government were offering very generous grants for agriculture in general. The emergence of supermarkets, which demanded national products supplied at a low price, also contributed to the decline of Cumberland sausage.

"Back in the '60s we'd be producing 20 or 30 pounds of sausage a day in our kitchen, we now talk in terms of tonnes per week," says Bar, "But tastes have changed over the years; now we're using only 50 per cent of sausage seasoning compared with pre-war tastes. If we used the amount we'd previously used it would just be too hot, tastes have become rather bland." This seems strange when Britain's favourite dish is supposed to be tikka masala!

Good Cumberland sausage is made by chopping pork, often the shoulder cut of the pig as it has a fair amount of fat, which is vital for the finished product. Chopping is preferred to mincing meat as chopping doesn't squeeze out moisture and arguably the rougher texture is an attraction. Pepper is added, plus the essential spices and a little salt for flavouring. Some butchers add rusk at this point. This mixture is then pushed through a nozzle and extruded into a casing, which is still made from pigs' intestines and is called hog casings. These are treated by soaking, turning inside out and scraping clean to make them suitable containers for the sausage. These natural casings are slightly porous which helps the sausages to cook without bursting. Cheaper imitations are sometimes made with synthetic casings which tend to stick in a frying pan.

(Strictly speaking the pig is the young animal and the older animal is a hog, regardless of gender, on becoming six to eight months old when it is old enough to mate.)

The traditional Cumberland sausage is fresh, has no links in the coil, does not require pricking with a fork and is best baked in an oven or grilled.

Great Orton butcher Jimmy Mulholland who with his wife Arline have been making Cumberland Sausage for forty years, buy in two sows each week specifically to make sausages.

Their product is 100 per cent meat with seasoning of salt and pepper plus two other ingredients that he won't divulge, but there is no rusk. "I used to go out to farms as a lad, butchering pigs on a Sunday and picked up my recipe from farmers. Every butcher has his own recipe," Jimmy states. They buy 'heavy' Landrace hybrid sows and use all the meat except the loin, which they cure to make bacon. Since Foot and Mouth hit Cumbria there has not been a pig auction and butchers now have to buy direct from farms. Jimmy Mulholland and his son Jimmy junior make their excellent Cumberland Sausage by cutting the meat by hand in chunks and seasoning it. It is then mixed thoroughly again by hand before mincing it once through a coarse mincer and finally extruded into natural casings in one long loop. "It fair flies out our door, so we must be doing summat reet" grins Jimmy senior.

Cured Sausage

The word sausage can be traced back to the Latin word "salus" meaning salted or preserved, yet Cumberland sausage is seldom made with preservative in it and only contains minute amounts of salt. It may be that our cold, wet English climate is to blame for the fact that historically we haven't produced cured sausages. Most of our sausages are made fresh to be eaten hot.

The British probably travel further than any other nation and those who are adventurous will have been introduced to sausages from other countries, many of which are eaten raw. One lad

Barry Shaw with his Solway Salami

from Silloth, Barry Shaw, travelled to Australia when he was first out of school and worked with a German butcher. He learnt enough to produce a modern version of a preserved sausage, which he calls Solway Salami.

Barry has been making a range of salami and chorizo for a few years. They vary in size, shape and flavourings. He uses mustard seed, cracked pepper and garlic to add to his pork to produce Solway Salami. The meat is chopped rather than minced, as in Cumberland sausage and mixed with spices and salt to preserve the finished salami. The meat is forced through a machine, excluding as much air as possible to prevent spoilage and is extruded through a nozzle into a natural casing. This process is done much more forcibly than when making Cumberland sausage as the salami is hung up to dry in a cool area for several weeks and no further cooking is required. The salami are sometimes smoked which adds to their flavour and keeping quality.

Traditionally, large Italian salami can lose up to fifty per cent of its weight as it dries, requiring the hanging string to be tightened during this period. A white bloom forms on the exterior of each salami caused by the harmless yeast cells which play a vital part in the maturing process.

Solway Brown Shrimps

The Solway Firth, dividing England from Scotland on the western border, is not known for particularly clement weather. In any season the sea can be rough with a strong wind; it can also look like a millpond and be freezing cold. As it is an estuary, the ebb tide often flows out over two miles from the shore uncovering thousands of mussels and starfish; the perfect diet for curlews, oyster catchers, gulls and other wading birds that make their home on the Solway.

Alfie Bennett has been fishing for Solway brown shrimps out of Silloth since he was a lad with his granddad. Today after more than a dozen years of commercial shrimping he goes out in all weathers and at all times. His working day is determined by the timing of the tides. Alfie owns two of the eight boats based in Silloth harbour. Alfie and his two sons, Paul and James and their cousin Darren keep the fishmonger in Silloth well stocked with fresh, frozen and potted brown shrimps.

Sailing out from the harbour, sometimes as far as the Isle of Man, Alfie and the boys decide where the fishing is at its best. Local knowledge is a great advantage when forecasting the location where shrimp are swimming. Brown shrimps live mainly along deep channels close to moving sand, where they feed on microscopic sea creatures.

Nets go over the side

The nets return full of shrimp

The nets are winched overboard and left to drag very slowly for about an hour.

The steel booms look like giant stabilisers, bring the nets back on the boat and depositing the catch onto the stern. Tiny shrimps are caught in hundreds of thousands along with an array of flat fish, crabs and jelly fish. Smaller flat fish and crabs are thrown back into the sea as they still have a chance of growing; but care is taken not to touch dangerous spiny weaver fish. Gulls fly behind the boats, opportunistically poised for their next meal.

Fresh seawater is used constantly to hose down the catch; sensibly Alfie and Darren are equipped with bright plastic overalls and boots. The small shrimps are put onto a trembling conveyer belt to

Annette lends a hand

Sifting the catch

Alfie Bennett cooks shrimp onboard

sieve out the larger fish, rinsed again and removed into large baskets.

A huge vat is ready on deck, with boiling saltwater into which the shrimps are dropped to be cooked instantly. You can't get much fresher than this, caught and cooked within minutes of being removed from the sea.

Cold sea water rinses them again before they're sifted and loaded into baskets ready for the gang of pickers who carefully remove the shells back on shore. This job is not as popular as it once was; machines are destined to replace people before too long.

Solway brown shrimps may be small, but they are tasty and have an interesting texture. Their

Returning to port

larger supermarket counterparts may have been factory farmed in south east Asia, depleting local drinking water supplies; then frozen, using energy that would be useful to the population and flown thousands of miles to fill our plates with flaccid pink prawns that have only slightly more taste and texture than watery blotting paper.

The tradition of potting shrimps (and other fish) has a long history, the practice having been primarily a preservation process whereby a spiced butter was poured over the top of the shrimps to eliminate air. With the coming of the railway, pots of buttered and spiced shrimps were transported to large urban conurbations. Today Alfie and his boys continue the trade and these delicacies are sold both locally and all over the country.

Dorothy picking shrimps

Solway Brown Shrimps

Beer

Beer is Britain's national drink. In recent years there has been a huge explosion in micro breweries, with more than a dozen in Cumbria and new breweries starting all the time. The Campaign for Real Ale needs to be credited with saving traditional British beer, which is now widely appreciated and has an international reputation. It is a natural product using natural ingredients. Within the brewing process there are obviously many variables which determine the beer style, characteristics and flavour. For example the fermentation process may take longer for a strong ale than a session bitter. The brewing process is roughly similar in all breweries; micro breweries thrive by creating interesting beer full of flavour and by paying attention to detail.

Barley is the grain that is the essential ingredient of British beer. A small number of British breweries have their own malt houses, but most breweries buy in malted barley. Malting is the process that turns the starch in barley into sugars. The barley is soaked for a couple of days in water, it swells and is then dried out on large floors where it is regularly aerated. Germination takes place with shoots breaking through the husk. After about a week it is transferred to a kiln room where heat stops germination. The amount of heat effects the malt characteristics; for a malt used in a mild (mild was once a popular drink in Cumbria) it will be heated to a higher temperature for longer giving a more 'burnt' taste.

Two types of malted barley

The malt is lightly crushed at the brewery to become grist and mixed with boiling water (known as 'liquor' in the trade) in a mash tun. After boiling and stirring for an hour or two it becomes wort, a thick, sweet porridgy liquid. The wort is run off into a boiler known as a copper. The remaining spent grain is sprayed or 'sparged', which ensures that all the natural sugars are captured and added to the copper.

The wort is boiled once again in the copper, hops are added at various stages of the boil and sometimes other 'adjuncts' are added to add flavour. When the boiling stage is completed the wort is cooled down, the hops are strained out and yeast is added and fermentation starts.

Yeast is a single cell micro-organism that turns the sweet sugary liquid into alcohol and carbon dioxide. Each brewery has its own yeast which has a significant role in the taste characteristics of a brewery's beer, some people consider it to be the 'signature' of a brewery. The strain of yeast used for beer is top fermenting, which creates a brown crust at the top of the fermenting vessel; lager yeast is bottom fermenting.

Fermentation takes about five days and then the beer is placed in conditioning tanks prior to putting it in casks or bottles. Real ale is still alive, in that the yeast is still slightly active which 'conditions' the beer and produces carbon dioxide. Cask beer have finings added which collect together the yeast material and proteins

Hops

Graeme Baxter adds ingredients to the mash tun

which then drop to the bottom, clearing the cask.

The role of hops is two-fold; flavouring and as a preservative. The most commonly used varieties in British brewing are Fuggles for their characteristic bitterness and Goldings for aroma. British beer is made with fertilised hops which are a rich source of aroma, flavour and character; lager is made with seedless hops.

Jennings is Cumbria's oldest brewery, founded in 1828 and moving to its present site in Cockermouth in 1874. It was recently bought by Wolverhampton and Dudley who say they are committed to keeping the brewery open; however there is concern relating to a number of its beers, in particular Jennings Dark Mild.

Coniston Brewing Company attracted national attention to Cumbrian brewing when they won what many consider to be the ultimate real ale award: the Campaign for Real Ale's Champion Beer of Britain in 1998 for Bluebird Bitter.

Peter and Carol Yates started Yates Brewery at Westnewton in 1986 and for the past eight years

Boiling water is added to the grist

Graeme and Caroline Baxter have continued the Yates brewing tradition. They use British-grown hops with intriguing names: Saaz, Goldings, Progress and Bramling Cross. As hop characteristics fluctuate with each harvest and age Graeme alters his recipes accordingly.

The malted barley which starts the brewing process comes from Lincolnshire. It varies in colour from golden to deep brown giving a range of flavours from light biscuit to burnt chocolate. As one might expect with an ingredient for brewing beer, the malted barley used by Yates has charismatic names: Maris Otter, Crystal and Cascade (which is compared to the smell of cat pee, but actually it gives a light citrus flavour).

It's amazing to discover that Peter Yates introduced the yeast in 1986 that Graeme still nurtures and uses today. Graeme believes that yeast plays as important a part of the beer making as hops, malted barley and water. "Our biggest fear is that wild yeasts in the atmosphere will infiltrate and infect our yeast. It's been going a long time and we've made over two thousand different brews from it." Spotlessly clean old curtains are thrown over each fermenting brew to cut out the chances of change in the yeast.

Caroline and Graeme Baxter

Yates produce a range of different beers including Yates Bitter, Fever Pitch, Solway Sunset and Sungoddess. Their logo is a wasp representing the sting in the tale of the taste. "It's a bit corny, I suppose", says Graeme, "and sometimes I wonder if the wasp is really a bee – we do make a honey beer called Bees Knees which is quite popular. We make four brews a week which is 36 barrels, giving us about 1200 gallons of beer."

Graeme is careful to weigh everything and although the brewery is small scale his attention to detail and timing is exact. "We want to make sure that there's consistency with our beer, so that when the publican puts it on the bar he can be confident the pint will be the same each time."

Fruit

Cumbria has a small number of commercial fruit growers, mainly producing soft fruit. A great source of fruit in season is domestic gardens and allotments. My own garden provides a number of fruits that are great to cook with or eat straight from the plant.

It is a coincidence that some of Cumbria's best apples grow along the Eden Valley. The River Eden passes the foot of the Pennines on Cumbria's eastern side where the weather may be cool and exposed. Contrary to some opinion, Cumbria's weather isn't always wet. Spring brings the wind, but insects still pollinate blossom and though summer may be short, it's always warm enough to ripen fruit.

Strawberry flowers

A northern collection of apple tree varieties is grown at Acorn Bank, near Temple Sowerby, which was gifted to the National Trust in 1950 and includes 186 acres of park and woodland. In their two and a half acres of orchard, many Cumbrian apple varieties thrive. With names such as Dunelow Seedling, Keswick Codlin, Norfolk Beefing, Blakeney Red and Scotch Bridget there is a wealth of apples for every season.

Historically a range of apples was grown to last from late summer, through winter and into spring. Cumbrian families would have been able to combine apples initially with soft fruit; then autumn berries and with the first harvest of rhubarb to make their traditional apple treats.

Apples are usually divided into two categories, cookers and eaters, but from my experience I've observed that cooking apples eat well when kept and I can cook the eaters! My Solway sprayed garden has two apple trees which are at least fifty years old; I've had these trees identified as Lane's Prince Albert, a hard dark green apple; and Monarch, both varieties from the 19th century. These are usually classified as cooking apples in that they are acidic and cook to a fluff. I've increased the range by planting another cooker, Newton Wonder which gives enormous fruit of a delightful orange to red hue, except where a leaf hides the skin and stops the sun from changing its colour. There is also a dwarf tree standing four feet tall which is prolific with the eating apple James Grieve. My parents told me it wouldn't grow this far north, so am pleased to have proved them wrong.

Jane Pollack inspects her apricots

Every October I wrap blemish-free cooking apples individually in newspaper and keep them in trays in an airy outbuilding. I have found that the Newton Wonder in particular stays firm and in good condition until February or March. The James Grieve doesn't keep and is worth eating straight from the tree for its crisp, fresh bite.

If a recipe calls for an apple to keep its shape, for example in an open apple tart, try using an eating apple which will be sweeter, requiring less added sugar. The traditional baked apple should be soft and fluffy but will need honey or sugar to bring out the flavour.

Along the River Eden from Acorn Bank is another fine garden, Winderwath, with many fruiting trees and soft fruits, belonging to Jane Pollack. The house and gardens were bought by Jane's family in the 1940s and it was Jane's mother Barbara who started the garden, the results of which are seen today.

Ron Davies has been Winderwath's head gardener since the 1980s growing organically within the one acre kitchen garden and producing a long season of crops with the help of a polytunnel and greenhouse. He's convinced that integrating 'loads and loads and loads of muck', along with his own compost and Lakeland Gold, contributes

Ron Davies, head gardener at Winderwath

to his success growing fruit. (Lakeland Gold is a bracken based soil conditioner made on a hill farm in the Lake District National Park.)

Ron maintains that pests are rare at Winderwath except for slugs, pheasants, pigeons and the house cat which brings in rabbits! He has contingency plans for them all, including large red and green discs on sticks to frighten pigeons. This seems to work.

The greenhouse which sits against a whitewashed, south-facing wall, is filled with nectarine, apricot and peach blossom in the spring and requires no extra heating to crop each fruit in the summer.

It is usually late summer and early autumn when cars appear to be abandoned in country lanes. The occupants are nearly always just a short walk away, carrying the ubiquitous plastic carrier bag, busily picking the ripening fruit in the hedgerows. The pickers may not be country folk, they are often urban dwellers who enjoy the abundant harvest of food for free in the summer.

Blackberries are known locally as brambles, once they have had a good soaking of rain followed by a sunny period the fruits are fat, luscious and ready to pick. In the wild area of our garden is a jungle of thorny brambles that delight us when the flowers blossom, offering hope of the crop to come. The best always seem to be just that bit further away

Jane Maggs

than arm's length. And in fact the lowest berry right at the tip of the stalk is the first to ripen and is generally the sweetest and fattest of all! Blackberries are the perfect partner for apples which ripen at the same time and can be used together in 'plate cakes' (the Cumbrian term for two layers of short crust pastry sandwiched with fruit), pies, crumbles, fools and summer puddings. Both blackberries and apples freeze well when combined.

Elderberries hang in the autumn like swollen hands with rich dark purple berries at the tips. Earlier in the year I find great delight when I am able to pick a few heads of the heavenly scented elder flowers to steep in water with lemons

Jane Maggs, Wild and Fruitful!

to make the year's first elderflower cordial. Sometimes the procedures get out of kilter, natural fruit yeasts ferment and cordial becomes 'champagne'. Elderflowers are famously matched with gooseberries to make jams and jellies with a flavour to resemble the Muscat grape. I found an old recipe for Elderberry and Apple jam written by hand from my Grandma, which I make every year. Rosehips, and haws from the hawthorn ripened red or orange can easily snare you with their prickles and spikes on every stem.

In the 1930s rosehips were found to contain more Vitamin C than any other fruit or vegetable, four times as much as blackcurrants and twenty times as much as oranges. After the Second World War the Solway Plain area with its thick, verdant hedgerows (which exist today) were a hive of activity as children were encouraged, and even paid, to pick rosehips. They were paid 2d per pound and took them into school for collection and delivery to the jam factory, where they were made into Vitamin C-rich rosehip syrup. This practice of rosehip picking continued well into the 1970s.

Jane Maggs is a keen picker of hedgerows and byways. She is vivacious and sunny, probably due to all the fresh air she gets whilst picking. Cumbrian hedgerows are ancient in parts, therefore supply a rich variety of fruiting plants. Jane keeps an eye on each prospective picking area during the year to determine whether any noxious sprays have been used.

But Jane doesn't have to rely purely on wild places for her fruit. Over the years since she started her company, Wild and Fruitful, she has grown a network of friends, neighbours, growers and gardeners throughout Cumbria, who produce wonderful fresh fruits without the need for unnecessary chemicals.

Jane is not an ordinary jam maker, she specialises in jams, jellies, curds, relishes, chutneys and fruit cheeses made from hand-picked, local fruits. She uses well-researched old recipes with the best of seasonal fruits. "Anyone can buy brambles from Romania," says Jane, "but that's not what I'm about!"

Jane lives in a solid, traditional Cumbrian red sandstone house, with purpose-built jam kitchen and storage areas. The six-ring cooker is constantly laden with giant saucepans, each bubbling gently.

She and her right-hand helper Jill Perry could be making anything from lemon curd, wild garlic and bramble jelly, damson jam or blackberry, elderberry and juniper jam, depending on the season. Between them they make small batches of each jam and jelly from hand picked fruit, hand-stirring each pan, filling the glass jars and hand labelling.

"The damson, ginger and green tea jam is a bit of a fiddle to make," says Jane "but I consider it the best to eat. I love making anything with raspberries, they're such a great fruit, wonderful colour and you just put them in the pot and boil them up. They have their own pectin so are easy to set. It's interesting to see what sells well and where. At the moment the Lavender Jelly is going like snow off a dyke, to quote a Cumbrian saying, but by next winter it could be the Plum, Almond and Amaretto Jam."

In 2003 Jane was voted North West Producer of the Year with her inspirational Hedgerow Chilli Jelly. She had wanted to make a 'Thai' type chilli sauce with local, wild ingredients because she loves chillies. Having spent seven years working around Australia she had become familiar with the variants and flavours of chillies and learnt to appreciate their usefulness. The resulting mixture of hips, haws and apples, combined with her favourite chillies finished with cider vinegar and sugar, impressed the judges sufficiently for Wild and Fruitful to win the title.

In the recipe section of this book there are a number of Wild and Fruitful preserves. The Rum Nicky had pear and ginger jam spread over the dates, and the Queen of Puddings uses the Damson, Blackberry, Plum and Elderberry jam giving a dark layer contrast to the meringue.

Damsons grow in hedgerows and gardens throughout Cumbria though not on any scale except in the southern valleys of Lyth and Winster. Although many people make it for themselves, Vicki and Oliver Barratt are the only people doing so commercially, using the traditional method with locally picked ingredients. Oliver and Vicki Barratt started Cowmire Hall Damson Gin in 1997, just after the Westmorland Damson Association was formed. At this time all the farmers in the Lyth and Winster valleys were encouraged to look after their damson orchards and to exploit them

Vicki Barrett with a freezer full of damsons

they soon progressed to purpose-designed premises, converted an underused farm building into the gin cellar, gradually purchasing proper tanks and other specialised equipment, such as bottling and labelling machines.

Many people in the Lyth and Winster valleys as well as other Cumbrians, myself included, make their own damson gin in the autumn. The traditional way is to fill a large, wide-necked jar about 3/4 full of damsons, add sugar and fill to the top with gin. Shaken daily, the gin will be ready by Christmas.

Oliver and Vicki do much the same, but in a 500 litre tank. As they cannot shake this up, they use a pump to circulate the liquid. They do several batches a year, so all damsons are frozen immediately on picking; this also breaks down the cell structure so that the flavour is released more easily. The Barratts have a gin specially blended for them that enables them to use less sugar in their recipe, which makes Cowmire Hall Damson Gin so delicious.

commercially. Having just got married they were looking for a farm diversification project. Making damson gin seemed an ideal way of commercially adding value to a traditional local fruit. Like most small food and drink enterprises, it started in the kitchen with their own fruit, and supermarket gin in two small drums, bottling with a funnel, and sticking on labels by hand.

Having no difficulty in selling their product,

Every spring the Lyth and Winster valleys are speckled white with damson blossom showing a promise of the next season's crop. Coming in from a wintertime walk and drinking Damson Gin in front of a log fire is one of life's great pleasures.

Fresh Water Fish

Char is one of the Lake District's indigenous fresh water fish, left over as a present from the Ice Age. Although isolated for several thousand years, it continues to thrive in lakes with deep, dark, cold waters.

In shape and size the char is similar to trout with a shiny greenish or bluish skin with numerous white spots. The male has some trace of orange or pink, more vivid in the spawning season when the whole fish turns vermillion. Each lake has its own season for char. The prime fishing times on Windermere are April and May; Coniston is slightly later in June and July, with Ennerdale, Buttermere and Crummock Water in the west of the county opening in July and August. Old time commercial char fishermen used to say,

"Bar Lad they'd take a flat iron in May" in other words, they were so easy to catch!

Albert Dixon was one of the last char fishermen on Windermere, giving up in the early 1960s. At this time he would have used long bamboo poles to fish, perhaps recycling the poles that carpets came wrapped around.

It is known that they used ten spinners spread out over different depths on the lines. They would have had a 'side of char tackle' either side of the boat doubling the chance of catching fish. Using different length spinners helped to identify the depth that fish were feeding at.

Eric Hope, who is a local fly casting instructor and fishing guide, gave me the opportunity to fish for char on Crummock Water in late August. He makes his own traditional char spinners, which historically have

Eric Hope

been made from beaten sovereigns. He chose the deepest region of the lake on a still, calm day to achieve my first catch.

At a measured hundred feet the water was amazingly clear considering the depth, with a dark peaty brown glimmer to it. The weather can determine the location of the fish; the char were where Eric had predicted they would be and I surprised myself by reeling in a beautiful, glistening silver and orange Artic Char. I was able to scoop a unique fish of the deep into my net. He was in excellent condition with all his gills intact, indicating that at ninety feet down his food source was plentiful (they feed partially on daphnia) and he was unstressed. A great wave of emotion prevented me from killing this particular fish and I was more than happy to slide it back into the water to swim another day.

Char has a delicate flavour, the flesh having a pale pink tinge. Char are best cooked quickly on each side in a hot buttered pan. Cumbria has a tradition of potting char. Some older recipes recommend simmering the fish for hours, often overnight, using the head, skin, bones and all. After which every bit of it was beaten down with butter, cream and mace before being placed it in

Fishing for char on Crummock Water

Hawkshead Trout Farm

a char pot. These pots are much sought–after collectors' items these days. The pots are round, made from white earthenware, the size of a small tea plate with curved sides, often decorated and some times with a lid. Melted butter would have been poured over the fish to seal out any air in order to preserve them. Considering how fine the flavour of these elusive fish is, it would seem like sacrilege to cook them beyond recognition and pound them like this.

In the south of Cumbria on Esthwaite Water, Nigel Woodhouse organically rears Rainbow Trout. At Hawkshead Trout Farm he started conventionally breeding trout in the mid-1970s to supply the summer hotel and restaurant trade.

He also sold at the farm gate for tourists to buy to take home; though this was small fry, if you'll excuse the pun, as the hotel trade grew rapidly. By the 1990s habits and tastes had changed and hotel demand declined and he was forced to sell to supermarkets. At this point Nigel realised that his business practices did not fit his aspirations and ideals. A major supermarket was buying his fish from Cumbria, processing it in Southampton or Motherwell and was selling it nationwide as Scottish trout. During a period of five years the supermarket increased their order but paid Nigel less. He was pushed into using any artificial aid or drug known to man to keep up. This was obviously unsustainable and Nigel reflects, "I couldn't stand it any longer, I realised I was

Annette and Nigel rowing out onto Esthwaite Water

Organic Trout from Esthwaite Water

NIgel Woodhouse's smoked trout

running a factory farm and I didn't like it. Before arriving in Cumbria I had followed organic principles in Cornwall growing courgette, sweetcorn, salad crops and flowers and it was the obvious solution to apply to my trout".

Nigel reduced the number of fish in each tank by 80 per cent, brought in pelleted organic food made from a by-product of fishmeal for human consumption and immediately the trout responded and he saw an improvement in their immune system.

His worry that the feed would deny his fish their pink flesh was unfounded. Non-organic feed has a pigment called astaxanthin added to it to make it pink. Esthwaite Water is rich in aquatic life and naturally well stocked with invertebrates, freshwater shrimp, which the fish enjoy eating to supplement their pellets, and their flesh is a good colour.

Nigel was inspired to try smoking trout after a trip to Finland, where smoked fish is popular. He set up a shed and began on a small scale. He was successful and has bought in more specialist equipment to smoke over a hundred fish at a time. He uses sustainable beech and oak wood sawdust for whole fish. The process is lengthy: putting the fish into brine for three hours, cold smoking them at 20 degrees for eight hours, followed by a hot smoking at 80 degrees for another three hours. The fillets go through a similar procedure, but as they are not so dense the brining and timing is much less.

Having perfected the practice he's now able to put fish through twice a week and smoked fillets of trout are one of his best sellers.

It took time and effort to get his fish certified organic, and he was the first person to obtain organic accreditation for fish in the world. That's quite a claim. With persistence Nigel has been instrumental in writing the standards and he's pleased that there are now enough organic fish producers to warrant their own association conference in Edinburgh. Spearheaded by the Soil Association, standards for rearing trout organically are being harmonised throughout Europe. Consumers aren't the only ones to benefit.

Esthwaite Water is primarily a coarse fishing lake. It is shallow and contains brown trout, pike and perch. Although Nigel considers the fish farm to be his core business and he says it's where his heart lies, he has brought about some diversification by introducing fly fishing on the lake. With his quiet and non-polluting electric boats people who want to fish have access to the waters. And if their best catch got away, they can always buy one of Nigel's perfect trout for tea.

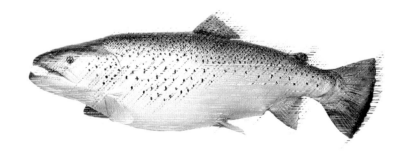

Wild Boar

Peter Gott is a businessman farmer with a passion for his animals and vision for the future. He farms at Sillfield Farm near Kendal, where he keeps pigs, rare breed Saddleback and Tamworth; other livestock includes some beef, sheep and deer, but his speciality is Wild Boar.

Wild Boar were hunted to extinction long ago in the British Isles, but demand for the meat resulted in Peter becoming one of a few farmers who have reintroduced them.

He has sixteen acres of woodland within his farmland in which his 150 wild boar roam. It is important to ensure that the Wild Boar

get used to Peter and accept him. He walks alongisde them in the woodland, giving them the occasional scratch. Some respond to their names and after a cry of 'pig, pig, pig', Boris, Aubrey or Hannibal can be seen trotting towards him. All but three of the herd are hand-friendly and this helps Peter to manage them safely.

Peter has a licence, not unlike a zookeeper's licence, that allows him to keep Wild Boar in natural surroundings where they are free to wander. The animals can travel three or four miles in a night, foraging as they go. They will eat practically anything, though they favour acorns in particular, Peter feeds them a balanced diet of barley, pea, wheat, and soya.

Peter Gott with his wild boar

Wild boar ham

The animals are slowly reared, letting nature take its course to increase numbers with just a little encouragement. The nineteen sows that make up the main breeding herd are put in with the boar in November each year. Peter maintains you could set your clock by their farrowing. The sows take themselves off into the woods to make a nest, and the young are born the following March and April. A litter averages out at four babies. In a good year Peter's wild boar will go for a successful second litter without any extra help.

"I take them to slaughter at eighteen months," says Peter, "but I have to shoot them myself at the slaughterhouse as the stun guns can't penetrate the hair." From there they are treated like red meat and the carcasses are hung for at least two weeks.

As his aim is to try and sustain his herd of Wild Boar, Peter is aware of the cost of their care and diet. "I like to get as much as I can back from my animals. I've spent a long time rearing them, so we cure practically every part to increase our return.

I can add value to the tune of £400 to £500 per animal by going down the curing route.

We've had to convince the Environmental Health people that we're doing it properly and it's only by persistence that we've succeeded. The legs are finished as hams and prosciutto, which we slice and packet; the shank end makes Wild Boar chorizo sausage. We use a dry cure and get bacon from the back and belly of the boar. Some bacon we smoke and ripen by hanging to mature for six to eight weeks. This is sold as pancetta, and what's left goes into sausage and pies." Christine Sleczka, Peter's partner makes the most wonderful hot-water crust pastry for a range of pies. Only the main collar joint of the wild boar is kept as a fresh joint and roasted to be sold ready sliced.

With his interest in meat and its processing throughout the world, it's hardly surprising that Peter initiated the Slow Food movement in Cumbria. This European-wide organisation was set up in Italy in 1986 to act as an antithesis to fast food. It promotes both regional produce, traditional recipes and sets value on taste and quality in food. Peter Gott comes from a sound starting point from which to launch these ideals.

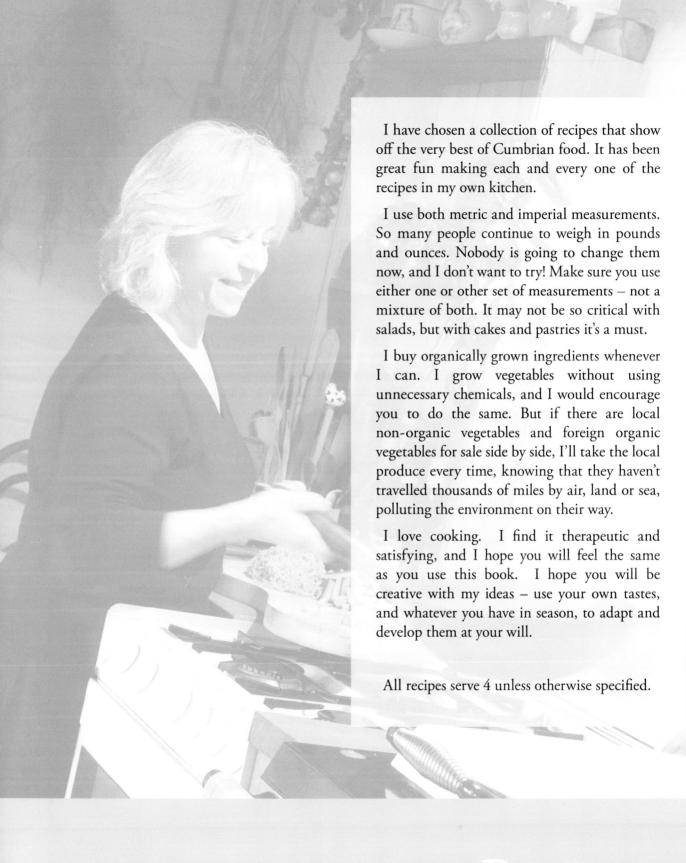

I have chosen a collection of recipes that show off the very best of Cumbrian food. It has been great fun making each and every one of the recipes in my own kitchen.

I use both metric and imperial measurements. So many people continue to weigh in pounds and ounces. Nobody is going to change them now, and I don't want to try! Make sure you use either one or other set of measurements – not a mixture of both. It may not be so critical with salads, but with cakes and pastries it's a must.

I buy organically grown ingredients whenever I can. I grow vegetables without using unnecessary chemicals, and I would encourage you to do the same. But if there are local non-organic vegetables and foreign organic vegetables for sale side by side, I'll take the local produce every time, knowing that they haven't travelled thousands of miles by air, land or sea, polluting the environment on their way.

I love cooking. I find it therapeutic and satisfying, and I hope you will feel the same as you use this book. I hope you will be creative with my ideas – use your own tastes, and whatever you have in season, to adapt and develop them at your will.

All recipes serve 4 unless otherwise specified.

Recipes

Pastry:

175g / 6 oz The Watermills 85% flour

75g / 3 oz butter

40g / 1½ oz smoked Cumberland cheese, grated

1 small free range egg, beaten

Filling:

1 large onion, finely sliced

1 red pepper, deseeded and cut into strips

2 tablespoons olive oil

75g / 3 oz fresh goat's cheese

salt and freshly ground black pepper

a little beaten egg

Goats Cheese Stumpies & Red Pepper Tarts

I tend to use 85% flour (see The Watermill at Little Salkeld) for this pastry as it adds fibre to the diet without being heavy. The pastry is quite short and crisp making the tarts a light starter or lunch dish but wholesome at the same time. Make the pastry first and leave it to relax while making the vegetable filling. I love the colour of the finished dishes. As the cheese doesn't melt, I like to brush each piece with a little beaten egg to brown the tops.

Thornby Moor Dairy, near Wigton make a fresh goats cheese called a Stumpie which is suitable for this dish.

Method

Make the pastry by sieving the flour into a bowl. Rub the butter into the flour using your finger tips until it resembles breadcrumbs. Stir in the finely grated smoked Cumberland cheese and the beaten egg to form a dough. Rest the dough in a cool place for about 20 minutes. Roll out the pastry to fill individual tartlets and bake them blind for 15 minutes. To bake blind I often use crumpled up foil placed in the pastry tartlet and cook in a preheated hot oven No. 7 / 220°C / 425°F for ten minutes, remove the foil and bake for another five minutes.

Heat the oil in a saucepan and cook the onion slices and red pepper for about 20 minutes until they are soft and browning. Season with salt and pepper and fresh oregano.

Fill each tartlet with a spoonful of the onions and peppers and top with slices of goat's cheese cut in quarters. Brush both the cheese and the edges of the pastry for a golden finish. Return the tarts to the oven for another 10 minutes to warm through and then serve with new potatoes and a green salad.

250g / 8 oz soft fresh goat's cheese

1 homegrown red chilli

2 tablespoons black olives

20ml / 2 tablespoons olive oil

1 tablespoon capers

1 teaspoon freshly ground black or pink peppercorns

2 fresh rosemary spears (length from your longest finger to your wrist)

The next three recipes involve preserving the contents in a sterilized jar. For this purpose place the washed jars in a hot oven for 10 minutes to dry them completely. Pour the hot relish into the hot jars and close immediately to create a vacuum.

One year I'd grown a glut of the red onions (Baron) and thought that they might not keep well but wanted to preserve them. Cumberland raspberry vinegar is a perfect foil for their sweetness. Try not to overcook this dish or you will loose the deep pinky red colour of the onions.

Chilli Cheese

I love to make pots of this Chilli Cheese to serve as a starter or use on a picnic, as well as to give as a present at any time of year. Excluding air by covering with olive oil preserves the cheese.

Use fresh chillies when you have them in the autumn and dried ones during the rest of the year. The dried ones will reconstitute to a softer texture on being kept.

The pots will keep better for being cool and airtight. Don't forget to bring the cheese to room temperature before eating to help the flavours come through.

Method

First consider how hot you want the cheese to be and decide whether to deseed the chilli or not. In any case cut it in fine slices, and always be careful not to touch your eyes after working with fresh chillies.

Mix the chilli, olives, olive oil, capers, pepper and rosemary. Cut the Stumpies into large diced pieces and place in a sterilised glass jar.

Pour the chilli oil over the top, cover and keep in the fridge overnight until well marinated. Serve with crusty bread to mop up the marinade. These will keep for some time (a month or longer) unless they get eaten in one go as they are so delicious. Once opened keep in the fridge.

6 medium sized red onions, sliced

2 tablespoons / 30ml sunflower oil

2 tablespoons brown sugar

2 tablespoons / 30ml Cumberland Raspberry Vinegar

1 bay leaf

1 tablespoon whole coriander berries – crush these a little to release their flavour

freshly ground black pepper and salt to taste

Red Onion Marmalade

This is a delicious relish that has a sweet and savoury taste. It looks gorgeous and is great to give as a present especially at Christmas as the peppers seem to sparkle through the glass jar. It's a great way to preserve a glut of pears – if you get one. Removing the seeds from the chilli pepper will soften the impact of the heat.

Method

Heat the oil and start to cook the sliced onions with the brown sugar, bay leaf and crushed coriander berries until they begin to soften. Add the vinegar and a little water if needed.

Cook this mixture until it is thick and soft. Taste to correct the seasoning. Cool slightly and pour into a couple of sterilised airtight jars to be kept in the fridge.

Excellent served with cold meats and cheese or stirred into a bean stew.

10 medium pears ripe but firm (don't peel them)

2 medium apples (don't peel them)

3 large onions, chopped

2 medium red peppers

1 fresh home grown red chilli (deseeding optional)

2 tablespoons salt

250g / 8 oz demerara sugar

½ pint (300ml/10 fl oz) cider vinegar

Pear And Pepper Relish

Method

Core the pears and apples and chop roughly. Trim, deseed and chop the peppers and slice the chilli.

Place all the vegetables in a glass bowl and sprinkle them with the salt. Leave this to stand for at least an hour. After one hour pour off the liquid and wash under cold water. Dry the vegetables on kitchen roll.

Bring the sugar and vinegar to the boil and simmer for 10 minutes to thicken slightly. Add the pears and vegetables. Bring to the boil again and cook gently for 15 minutes.

In the meantime sterilize the jars and bottle the relish when it is thick enough. Label and cool before storing.

Solway salami is made using mustard seed and works really well in salad with the raspberry vinegar dressing. Don't bother buying tomatoes in the winter as they are grown in water with no strength of sun to ripen them – wait for the local ones that have been grown for flavour to get a really tasty salad.

2 Solway salamis, cut into diagonal slices

½ red onion, sliced very thinly and separated into rings

2 tomatoes, deseeded and finely diced

4 tablespoons / 40ml extra virgin olive oil

1 tablespoon / 10ml raspberry vinegar

enough washed green leaves to cover the base of your salad platter - sorrel, spinach or little gem lettuce, baby beetroot leaves or lambs lettuce

salt and pepper to taste

Solway Salami Salad

Method

Mix the salami, onion and tomatoes together gently. Make a dressing by mixing the oil and vinegar and season well. Toss the salami salad in the dressing and serve on a bed of green leaves.

Starters, Preserves & Salads

Crisp Baked Brown Shrimps

250g / 8 oz brown shrimps

black pepper

150ml / 5 fl oz soured cream

fresh breadcrumbs

50g / 2 oz unsalted butter

fresh parsley

A simple dish which brings out the individual flavour of brown shrimps contrasted with the texture of the cream and breadcrumbs. Serve this as a starter or light lunch with a crisp salad. The shrimps may be small but are full of flavour and texture, far better than pale pink watery prawns.

Method

Butter 4 ramekins and spoon about 2 tablespoons brown shrimps into each. Season thoroughly with freshly ground black pepper and cover each one with soured cream.

Sprinkle a thin layer of breadcrumbs over the cream and dot with small knobs of butter.

Bake in the centre of a preheated oven Gas 5/190°C/375°F for 10 minutes. Finish the shrimps under a hot grill for a minute or two until the breadcrumbs are golden brown.

Garnish each dish with parsley and lemon then serve with chunks of warm wholemeal bread and butter.

Hawkshead Smoked Trout Paté

1 packet Hawkshead Organic Smoked Trout (about 250g)

1 thumb-length of cucumber

1 organic lime

1 tablespoon natural yogurt

1 tablespoon fresh chives

salt and freshly ground black pepper

I first made this paté one summer after visiting the Trout Farm on Esthwaite Water. I knew the subtle taste of trout would require light, fresh ingredients and as it was summer, chives and cucumber were in abundance. Serve with crusty Granarius bread.

Method

Wash and zest the lime, retaining the zest in a bowl.

Wash and grate the cucumber into another bowl, then squeeze out the juice from the grated cucumber.

Break up the trout and place it into the bowl with the cucumber. Squeeze half the lime into this and mix it all together to create a textured mass. Add the natural yogurt and a little of the lime zest to get a soft consistency. Season lightly and mix well.

Wash and finely chop the chives and add this to the trout. Mix again and transfer to a serving dish, using the half lime and extra cucumber slices to garnish the finished dish.

Starters, Preserves & Salads

4 Hungarian wax peppers

100g / 3½ oz cream cheese

1 tablespoon fresh parsley, finely chopped

2 spring onions, cut into thin slivers

Herbed Cheese Stuffed Peppers

Rose Wolfe grew these delightful peppers one year and gave me a large bowlful. The sweetness of the peppers is highlighted by grilling the skins until they are black. With fresh parsley and perpetual spring onions from the garden they came together as the right combination.

Method

Cut the peppers in half lengthways straight through the stem. Remove the seeds and put the peppers skin side up under a hot grill until the skin has blackened. Put the peppers immediately into a bowl and seal with cling film before leaving them to cool.

Mix the cream cheese with the parsley and spring onions.

Remove the blackened skin from the peppers. Take each skinless half pepper still with its stalk and place one full teaspoon of the cream cheese on the inside flesh. Roll up the stuffed pepper from the pointed end and place on a serving platter with stalks sticking up.

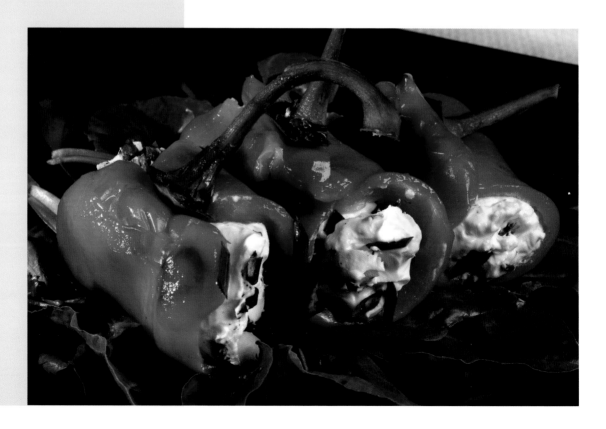

Starters, Preserves & Salads

Herdwick Liver Paté

450g / 1 lb Herdwick livers

125g / 4 oz butter

1 onion, finely chopped

1 clove garlic, sliced

2 bay leaves

bouquet garni

2 or 3 tablespoons damson gin to taste

This recipe came about as I was demonstrating cooking with Herdwick meat at a local summer show. I was concerned about using the liver knowing that it has a strong flavour that may be dominant. My usual paté recipe includes brandy as the alcohol but I thought that Herdwick would be too strong with brandy. Cowmire Hall Damson Gin was just the answer. It brings a sweetness to the savoury mix and judging by the response of the people who tried it while the rain fell in torrents, I'd made a good local decision.

Method

Heat half the butter in a large pan and soften the onion and garlic with the lid on.

Clean and pat dry the livers and remove any gristle. Cut into small chunks. Add these to the pan and stir well to cover with the buttery onions. Place the bay leaves and a bouquet garni in with the meat and stir well then leave to simmer for another 5-8 minutes until the liver is cooked through.

Remove from the heat and cool slightly. Remove the bouquet garni and bay leaves.

Blitz the mixture until smooth blending in the remainder of the butter and 2 or 3 tablespoons damson gin.

Place in a suitable serving dish and garnish with parsley. Eat with hot crisp buttermilk bread.

Starters, Preserves & Salads

5 tablespoons gram flour

1 large onion, sliced

pinch of salt

1 medium courgette, sliced

1 teaspoon ground cumin

1 tablespoon fresh coriander leaves, chopped

sunflower oil

¼ cucumber, grated

2 tablespoons natural yoghurt

1 tablespoon or more fresh mint leaves, chopped

Courgette Pakora With A Cucumber And Mint Dip

Gram flour is made from chickpeas. It is high in protein and useful for people who can't eat wheat products.

When my children were small they would come home from primary school ravenously hungry and I would enjoy making Pakora for them. They would call the Pakora 'vegetarian crab' because the onion slices turn like crab claws in shape.

Children love eating them with their fingers, dipping them into a cucumber and yogurt sauce. Any vegetable can be used in the Pakora – try carrots or mushrooms. I've even resorted to tinned sweetcorn when there really isn't anything fresh available.

Method

Put the flour, cumin, salt and fresh coriander leaves into a bowl and stir well. Add the sliced onion and courgette with enough water to form a thick, creamy paste.

Have ready a small pan with 1" of the sunflower oil. Get it hot. Have ready an ovenproof dish with kitchen paper to drain the pakora.

Take a spoonful of the mixture and put it into the hot oil. Let it 'set' and brown slightly before turning. Cook the other side and drain on the kitchen paper. Cook the pakora a few at a time until all the mixture is used.

Serve hot with the cucumber and yogurt dip. Grate the cucumber, squeeze out any excess liquid and mix with natural yoghurt, freshly ground black pepper and fresh chopped mint.

Green Herb Salad

1 crisp green hearty lettuce or variety of fresh leaves such as sorrel, cos lettuce, baby beetroot leaves, young spinach leaves

½ cucumber, thinly sliced

1 stick celery, chopped

100g (small bunch) grapes, cut in half

1 tablespoon fresh mint leaves removed from the stem, roughly torn

1 tablespoon green fennel fronds, roughly torn

1 tablespoon parsley, roughly torn

1 tablespoon chives cut in thin diagonal pieces

Dressing:

3 tablespoons (30ml) olive oil

1 tablespoon (10ml) cider vinegar or lemon juice

1 teaspoon Cumberland mustard

1 teaspoon Cumbrian runny honey

salt and pepper to taste

1 clove of garlic, crushed

I always feel heartened to know that spring is on its way when chives are once again visible in the soil and the tarragon suddenly sprouts up. This is the time to use chives at their best whilst still succulent and tender. Once the pretty mauve chive flowers have arrived use them on top of the salad as well.

Method

Wash and lightly dry the salad leaves and place in a large bowl or platter. Scatter the cucumber, celery and grapes over the top and sprinkle over a selection of the fresh herbs. Make the dressing by whisking the vinegar, Cumberland mustard and honey together, then whilst still stirring add the oil. Crush the garlic into this and season with the salt and pepper. Drizzle this dressing over the salad just prior to serving.

240g / 8 oz small cabbage (red or white)

1 small red onion

1 eating apple, leave the skin on

1 baby leek, washed

Dressing:

3 tablespoon olive oil

1 tablespoon Cumberland raspberry vinegar,

½ teaspoon Cumberland organic wholegrain mustard

Winter Salad

Just because it's winter doesn't mean we can't eat raw, fresh foods.

The red and white hard cabbages are at their best in the winter months and blend well with apple and leek. The crunch of Cumberland wholegrain mustard marries the sweetness of apple and red onion and there's no need for salt and pepper!

Method

Prepare the vegetables by dicing the apple, finely slicing the leek and shredding the cabbage finely into a large bowl. Make up the dressing by placing the mustard into a small bowl, then add the vinegar until the mustard is blended. Slowly whisk in the olive oil until the dressing is thick. Pour the dressing over the salad. Toss the salad and serve either on its own with crusty bread or with meat or fish dishes.

Summer Soup

250g / 8 oz (large handful) broad bean tops

1 large onion, finely chopped

1 carrot, finely chopped

250g / 8 oz new potatoes, washed and diced but not peeled

1 tablespoon butter

900g / 1½ pints vegetable stock or water

shelled broad beans

seasoning of salt and freshly ground black pepper

cream to serve

I love to grow broad beans. On warm summer evenings the perfume of their flowers is beyond description – I could sit amongst them and watch the sun go down. They are a very versatile vegetable and the pods can be eaten whole when still very young. The beans freeze well for winter use and if left on the bush until too large, the beans can be double podded and used in soups and patés. It is the tops of the growing bushes that I use to make this next soup. Each handful is a lush green with a subtle flavour of the broad bean and makes a wonderful creamy soup served hot or cold in the summer.

Another advantage of pinching out the tops for the soup is that it helps the broad beans to mature and stops black fly from attacking.

Method

Heat the butter in a heavy pan and put in the chopped onion and washed, chopped broad bean tops. Cook for about 5 minutes until all is softened.

Add the chopped carrots and potatoes and continue to stir well while cooking. Put a lid on the pan and sweat the ingredients for 10 minutes over a low heat. Shake the pan from time to time during cooking. Add the stock or water and seasoning and stir well. Cook for 15 minutes until softened. Add the shelled broad beans and cook for a final 5 minutes so that they retain their colour. Check the seasoning and mash slightly or purée as desired. Serve with a swirl of cream in each bowl.

Starters, Preserves & Salads

Garlic Family Soup

6 leeks

2 medium onions, peeled

6 shallots

1 head garlic cloves, peeled and halved

4 tablespoons extra virgin olive oil

Bouquet garni:

750g / 1½ lbs potatoes, peeled and cubed

fresh herbs: parsley, tarragon, chives etc

There's no getting away from it – I love garlic, and onions, and leeks and, in fact all the edible alliums. This is a superb soup to make in the autumn when all the ingredients are at their best. And have no fear – the cooking dissolves any long term strength of the garlic so that you end up with a glorious tasting creamy soup.

Method

Trim and wash the leeks, separating the coarse dark green parts from the white. Chop the white and pale green portions.

Make a leek broth by combining the dark green leeks, a pinch of salt and 3 litres water and bring this to the boil. Cover and simmer for 15 minutes.

Slice the onions thinly. In a heavy based saucepan combine the white parts of the leeks with the onions, shallots, garlic, olive oil, bouquet garni and salt. Let this sweat, covered for 10 minutes over a moderate heat.

Strain the leek broth and pour it over the vegetables. Add the cubed potatoes and bring this to a simmer. Cover and cook for 1 hour. Remove and discard the bouquet garni. Purée the soup. Serve in warmed soup bowls garnished with fresh herbs.

Starters, Preserves & Salads

Bouquet Garni

Although this is a French term, it is widely used to describe a little bundle of herbs used to flavour soups and stews. There is always a piece or two of celery lurking at the bottom of the fridge, perfect for the job. Making your own means you don't have to buy highly salted stock cubes.

Method

Take two large pieces of fresh celery.

Fill the bottom celery piece with fresh thyme, parsley stalks...

... and a bay leaf.

Place the other piece of celery on top.

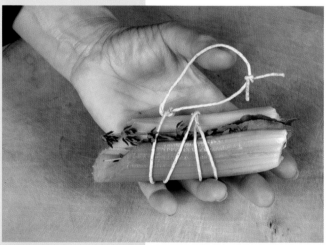

Tie up with kitchen string and the completed bouquet garni is ready to go into the pot.

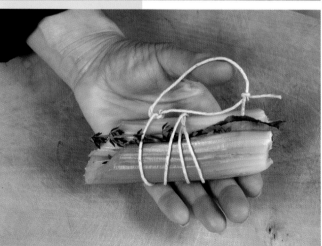

Bouquet garni adding flavour to the vegetables cooking in the pan for stocks, soup or stews.

Don't forget to remove the parcel before serving! When the bouquet is cool, squeeze it to remove the very last of the flavoursome juices and throw the remains on the compost heap.

4 venison steaks

30 ml / 2 tablespoons
Cumberland raspberry
vinegar

15 ml / 1 tablespoon game
or beef stock, or plain water
if you have no stock

2 tablespoons cold butter

2 tablespoons freshly
chopped parsley

seasoning

Pan-fried Venison Medallions

Organically farmed local venison is consistently tender with great flavour and is the perfect quick fry meat that cooks in minutes for serving with a seasonal salad. The fruity vinegar used to deglaze this dish makes a good foil for the richness of the meat.

Method

Dab the steaks with kitchen paper before placing in a preheated, very hot pan which has been brushed with a little olive oil before heating.

Pan-fry the venison for about 2 minutes either side depending on the thickness of the steak and how pink you like it cooked. Put the steaks on a warmed serving dish.

Place the pan over a lower heat and swirl in a couple of tablespoons of raspberry vinegar to deglaze the pan. Add the stock or water and reduce this for a few minutes until it is thick and syrupy. Add a few knobs of cold butter and fresh parsley, whisk these in the pan until well mixed and pour over the steaks. Buttered new potatoes and a crisp salad make up a perfect summer lunch.

pan fried venison served here with Damson Chilli Sauce

Roast Venison With Juniper

1 strip loin of venison

1 tablespoon juniper berries

salt and freshly ground black pepper

olive oil

Juniper can be found growing wild in Cumbria. But beware, the bushes are very prickly! I love the combination of flavours here and find that the venison takes on sufficient of the juniper flavour for it still to be apparent when eaten cold.

Method

Preheat the oven to Gas 8/230°C/450°F

Lightly crush the juniper berries using a pestle and mortar or rolling pin. Place a tablespoon of oil in a roasting tin and put on the top of the cooker over a low flame to heat the oil. Put the juniper berries on a chopping board and roll the venison over the berries so that they coat the meat. Season the meat with salt and pepper and place it in the hot roasting tin. Be careful as you seal the meat to cook it quickly on each side, as it may spit. Baste if necessary to keep it oiled. Turn off the heat and place the roasting tin in the oven and cook for about 15 to 20 minutes depending on whether you prefer your meat to be pink. Rest the meat, covered, for at least 15 minutes if you are eating it hot, or let it cool and then slice thinly. A good dark fruity relish, such as Damson Chutney, goes well with venison.

Main Course

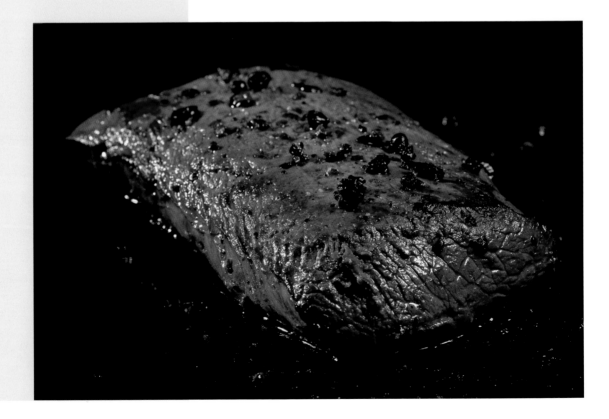

Cumberland Sausage

450g / 1 lb good quality Cumberland Sausage

1 glass red wine

at least 3 long sprigs fresh rosemary

2 tablespoons stock

Cumberland Sausage is probably the best known Cumbrian dish and the one that is most often eaten. The easiest way of cooking it is to place it on a rack in a roasting tin and cook in the oven on a moderate heat until golden. Here, however, I've used the frying pan and cooked it with wine.

Method

Take the sausage and coil it tightly into a spiral. Pierce the rosemary sprigs through the diameter of the sausage so that it's held solid and can be turned without breaking. Ease the sausage apart slightly so that there is a space between the coils for even cooking.

Place the sausage in a frying pan with its own lid on top of the cooker. Cook over a medium heat until the sausage turns brown. Any fat that runs from the sausage can be poured off. Using tongs, turn the sausage over to cook the other side and let this brown. Pour off any further fat.

Pour the red wine over the sausage and place the lid on the pan to continue cooking.

Add a few tablespoons of water if it looks as if it's going dry before being thoroughly cooked. Cook until the wine evaporates and the sausage is completely cooked. It will have turned a deep red colour as it has absorbed the wine.

Remove the sausage to a preheated serving dish and deglaze the pan with the stock and use this to serve with the sausage with lots of creamy mashed potato.

Main Course

Salt Beef In Yates Bitter Beer

900g / 2 lb silverside or salmon cut of beef

12 allspice berries

50g / 2 oz coarse salt

12 black pepper corns

3 bay leaves

3 cloves garlic

1 teaspoon saltpetre (optional - this is available at some smaller chemists)

2 tablespoons soft brown sugar

For the oven:

600ml / 1 pint Yates bitter beer

1 teaspoon cloves

1 teaspoon black pepper

1 onion, unpeeled and chopped

1 celery stalk, broken in places

1 carrot, roughly chopped

4 parsley stalks, broken in places

This Salt Beef recipe probably goes back hundreds of years in one form or another. I love to make it at Christmas or for special celebration buffets as it looks as good as it eats. You need to start the beef off at least one week before the meal.

Method

Using a sharp knife, pierce the flesh of the meat to help the marinade develop within the meat.

Mix the salt and the saltpetre together. Crush the leaves, spices and garlic in a pestle and mortar and mix well before rubbing this over the meat. Cover the meat loosely and turn it every day in this mixture for one week, keeping it in the fridge or a cold pantry. Juices will run from the meat and they should be basted over the piece every day.

After 7 days, wash the meat and put it into a large oven-proof dish with the other ingredients:

Once all the other ingredients are in with the meat, cover with cold water, put on a lid or foil covering and cook for 1-1½ hours. Pressure cooking reduces this cooking time considerably. Leave the meat to go cold in the liquid. Once the meat is cold, it will have shrunk. Slice very thinly and serve cold as part of a buffet table with seasonal salads.

Main Course

900g / 2 lb Herdwick shoulder

1 whole black pudding (usually about 350g / 12 oz in weight)

1 tablespoon sunflower or other light oil

600ml / 1 pint hot water or stock

1 bayleaf

900g / 2 lb potatoes, sliced

350g / 12 oz onions, coarsely chopped

4 carrots, peeled and roughly chopped

salt and freshly ground black pepper

Cumberland Tatie Pot

Cumberland Tatie Pot (tatie rhymes with matey) is a satisfying dish that can be left to cook in the oven all day if need be. A few years ago we had a surprise party in our village hall for a much loved lady and a few of us made a Tatie Pot each. The resulting meal was stunningly different. One neighbour's traditional recipe had both lamb and beef in it, another lamb and mint, and mine was the one below. All of them had the vital ingredient of black pudding. Each was eaten with gusto and of course served with pickled red cabbage.

Method

Layer the meat, onions, carrots and slices of black pudding in a suitable ovenproof dish. Add the bayleaf and thyme and pour over the water or stock seasoned with salt and black pepper.

Arrange the potato slices on top, overlapping them like slates on a roof. Season with salt and pepper and add a few flecks of butter on top.

Cover with foil and cook near the top of the preheated oven Gas 6/200°C/400°F for about 90 minutes. Remove the foil and cook for a further 45 minutes to 1 hour until browned on top. Traditionally served with pickled red cabbage.

2 tablespoons olive oil

salt and pepper

2 onions, cut into bite-sized chunks

1 bulb garlic, broken into cloves

4 carrots, cut into bite-sized chunks

2 racks Herdwick lamb

Hazel's Hot As Hell Rack Of Herdwick With Roasted Garlic And Vegetables

With Herdwick having such health giving properties – the fat is said to contain omega 3 – this dish is a great favourite. I like to serve it as a simple dinner party main course that can be prepared well ahead of time and cooked as the starters are being eaten.

It is named after Hazel Relph, who with her husband Joe breeds Herdwick Sheep in the Borrowdale valley.

Method

Place all the prepared vegetables cut into one-inch chunks in a roasting tin and season well. Mix with one tablespoon of the olive oil and leave to stand.

Take the Herdwick racks score the fat, season the meat and rub in the remaining olive oil. Place them on top of the vegetables.

Place in a preheated very hot oven Gas 9/240°C/475°F for about 30 minutes. You may need to lift the meat during the cooking to give the vegetables a stir, but the resulting crisp fat will have cooked the veggies beneath the tender meat.

Leave the meat to rest before carving into slices. Serve with redcurrant jelly and the cooked vegetables.

Main Course

1 x 3 or 4 ribs of British Beef

salt and pepper

Roast Rib Of Beef

There can be nothing more traditional than a roast beef made with the fore rib of the beast. It looks stunning when brought to the table to be carved and it cooks very evenly.

Method

Remove the beef from the fridge one hour before roasting so that the joint comes up to room temperature. Weigh the joint to calculate the cooking time. For joints on the bone cook for 15 minutes per pound weight plus 15 minutes (equivalent to 30 minutes per kilo plus 30 minutes). For joints already boned and rolled, cook for 20 minutes to the pound plus 20 minutes, or 40 minutes per kilo plus 40 minutes.

Preheat the oven to Gas 7/220°C/425°F. Place the beef in a roasting tin with the fat side uppermost, season the joint well and place in the oven. Baste every 20 minutes or so with the fat that has oozed from the meat. Once cooked the fat should be crisp and browned. Leave the joint to rest for about 15 minutes before carving. I find it best to place the meat on the carving board and cover it lightly with foil for the resting time.

This usually gives me time to get the Yorkshire puds in the oven. Make up the mixture once the meat has gone in the oven which gives it time for the flour to be well absorbed. The second whisking with cold water helps to make light and crisp puddings. As children Mum would always make a few extra which we relished with syrup for tea time.

Main Course

125g / 4 oz plain flour

pinch salt

1 free range egg

150ml / ¼ pint milk

Yorkshire Puddings

Method

Sift the flour and salt into a bowl or jug and crack the egg into this. Using a whisk slowly add the milk until the mixture is thick and bubbly. Leave this to stand for at least one hour.

Using some of the fat from the beef roast, heat one teaspoon of fat in the individual pudding tins. Get this fat really hot before you add the mixture. Make sure that the oven is preheated to Gas 7 / 220˚C / 425°F.

Rewhisk the batter vigorously adding about 1/4pint cold water.

Pour a little into each of the pudding tins and place in the oven immediately. Cook for 15-20 minutes until each pudding is golden and risen.

A Note On The Gravy

To make really good gravy use the residue that has been left in the roasting pan. Heat this pan slowly on the top of the cooker and then while still stirring, add two tablespoons of flour and mix well. This should take up all the fat and goodness of the meat and turn a golden brown colour. Add hot vegetable water or stock to create a smooth sauce (if it goes lumpy, remove it from the heat and use a blitzer).

Season with a little soy sauce and black pepper and a glassful of good red wine.

450ml / ¾ pint double cream whipped

2 tablespoons grated fresh horseradish

½ teaspoon sugar

½ teaspoon salt

2 teaspoons vinegar

1 teaspoon made Cumberland mustard

1 tablespoon white breadcrumbs

Horseradish Sauce

If you grow horseradish and would like to prepare your own sauce, here is a recipe. Dig up a root of horseradish, wash and peel it. It may be easier to grate it from frozen. Do be careful with the horseradish root as it's hot and pungent.

Method

Mix all ingredients together and serve with roast beef, smoked mackerel or other

smoked fish. Keep the sauce in a clean glass jar in the fridge and it will last for weeks.

1 large onion

2 carrots, peeled and chopped roughly

350g / ¾ lb cold roast beef or lamb

120ml / 4 fl oz gravy

450g / 1 lb mashed potatoes

Shepherd's Pie (made with cold roast lamb) or Cottage Pie (made with beef)

Always use cold roast meat for this dish. The flavour of the meat that has been previously roasted is far superior to fresh mince and the added advantage is that it's a great way to use up left over meat and gravy. It was a tradition in my parents' house to eat Cottage Pie on a Monday after the Sunday roast and one that we looked forward to. The quantities are approximate but give you good proportions.

Method

Mince the beef and onion together or chop very finely. Place in a saucepan with the carrots and mix with the gravy. Bring to the boil and simmer for 15 to 20 minutes. Taste for seasoning if necessary. Add a little red wine if you need to thin this down.

Peel, cook and mash the potatoes with butter to make them smooth.

Place the hot beef into an ovenproof serving dish and top with the creamy mashed potatoes. Using a fork, fluff up the potatoes to make a pattern. Put a little butter on the top and place under a preheated grill until golden brown. Serve immediately with fresh green vegetables.

3 pork chops

salt and pepper seasoning

Red Gooseberry sauce:

450g/1lb homegrown red gooseberries taken from the freezer and thawed

1 small onion

2 red chillies (remove the seeds and white membrane if you don't like dishes too hot)

2 cloves garlic, peeled

1 tablespoon unsalted butter

2 tablespoons brown sugar

Grilled Pork Chop With Red Gooseberry Sauce

This next recipe came about as a mistake! I was about to film a programme of Home Grown for Border Television and had prepared all my ingredients the night before. But I had delved into the deep freeze to take out frozen plums in a dim light last thing at night, and in the morning I found that the plums were in fact red gooseberries. The variety was Wynham's Industry grown by Keith Tibbott of Southwaite; they are sweeter than the green variety and made an excellent sauce with the pork chop. I've also used the same sauce recipe substituting damsons for the gooseberries and serving it as an accompaniment for venison steaks. In this case remove the damson stones before cooking and if they've been frozen the stones will come away easily.

Method

Season the chops with salt and pepper and place in a preheated hot oven or under a preheated grill. Cook for approximately 10 minutes depending on the thickness of the meat, turning once during the cooking. The chop is done when the fat is crisp, the meat is tender and the juices run clear.

For the sauce, heat the butter in a heavy frying pan and add the chopped onion and chillies, cooking them until they are softened. Mix in the crushed garlic and the fruit. Bring the mixture to the boil and simmer for a few minutes. Do not overcook as the sauce will discolour. Taste for seasoning, adding the sugar and a little salt if you think you need it. Serve to accompany the crisp chops with at least one green vegetable and some potatoes or rice.

Main Course

1 large onion, finely sliced

750g / 1½ lb pork fillet, cut in slices

1 large cooking apple, sliced but not peeled

75g / 3 oz butter

1 tablespoon sunflower oil

5cm / 2" piece of fresh root ginger, peeled and grated

Fillet Of Pork Slices With Apples And A Butter And Ginger Sauce

The fillet of any animal is tender because as a muscle it sits next to the backbone and does very little physical work, unlike the fore quarters. The harder a muscle has had to work the longer it requires to be cooked. Pork fillet is versatile and quick to cook but often needs a piquant sauce. I love the combination of apples and butter at the best of times, and here with ginger it works well with the pork.

Method

Heat half the butter in a large pan and cook the onion slices until softened (this may take 20 minutes). Remove the onions to a plate, leaving a little butter in the pan and add the sunflower oil. Bring the pan up to a high heat and quickly cook the pork slices until brown. Remove these to a warmed serving dish. Slide the onions back into the pan, add the ginger and apple slices, and cook gently for about 5 minutes. Try not to break up the apples. Add a little more butter and stir until it is melted into the sauce. This may need a tablespoon or more of water depending on the juiciness of the apples. Spoon the onions and apples on top of the pork and pour over the melted butter with ginger to serve. This needs at least one crisp green vegetable or salad and new potatoes to mop up the juices.

Main Course

2 large onions, chopped finely

2 English eating or cooking apples, grated

2 free range eggs

125g / 4 oz fresh breadcrumbs

2 lemons (grated zest and juice)

1 heaped tablespoon chopped fresh sage

700g / 1½ lb Cumberland sausage meat

150g / 6 oz chopped cooked chestnuts (tinned or vacuum packed if you can't get fresh)

salt and pepper

red-skinned apple to garnish

Cumberland Sausagemeat And Apple Loaf

This meat loaf is particularly good in the autumn when apples are plentiful and sage is still with us. I have frozen the completed loaf successfully so it's worth making at least double when you've got the flavour that you like. Ask your butcher for Cumberland Sausagement that is lean and coarsely cut.

Method

Place all ingredients (except the red-skinned apple for garnish) together in a large mixing bowl and blend together.

Core and thinly slice the red apple and put it in the base of the prepared loaf tin to form a pattern, then place the sausagemeat mixture on top, press well down to exclude any air and cook in a preheated oven Gas 4/180°C/350°F for 30 minutes until the loaf is cooked. Serve on a warmed plate with fresh steamed green vegetables. Can also be eaten cold.

250g unbleached white flour or 85% flour

2 free range medium sized eggs

Pasta With Leek And Cream Sauce

When my "girls" are laying well during the summer months it gives me enormous satisfaction to make my own pasta. The colour of the finished pasta is rich due to the hens having a varied diet and laying gloriously deep-coloured eggs.

I bought a pasta maker when my daughter Laura was young and we made lots of mess in the kitchen involving flying flour and odd shapes to make fresh pasta. Once you've eaten it fresh the dried stuff will wane into obscurity for taste and texture. Don't bother adding oil to the cooking water, simply stir well during the first minute of cooking and the pasta won't stick together.

Method

Sift the flour onto a clean work surface and make a well in the middle of the flour. Crack the two eggs into this well and using a fork, whisk to amalgamate the eggs with the flour. Continue working until a soft dough is formed, using your hand to bring it all together. Leave the dough to rest in a cool place, covered in cling film or a clean, wet tea towel for at least 30 minutes. Roll out using lots of flour to keep it all dry. Cut or use a pasta mill to shape.

Bring a large pan of salted water to the boil and whilst at a rolling boil plunge the pasta into the water and stir. Cook uncovered for about 2 minutes when the pasta will rise to the surface.

Drain and serve immediately with your favourite vegetable sauce. My personal easy favourite is to cut fresh washed leeks into large diagonal slices and soften them in melted butter. After 5 minutes add the drained pasta and a small pot of sour cream, season with salt and pepper and mix well. It really couldn't be simpler.

Main Course

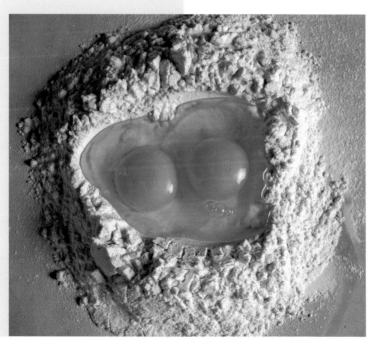

Fennel Baked Trout

4 fresh trout, cleaned

75g / 3 oz butter

1 organic unwaxed lemon

handful of fresh green herb fennel, washed

salt and freshly ground black pepper

As a rule I would say cook fish quickly and simply. However this whole trout is baked in the oven and does need at least 20 minutes. In fact cooking it longer is an advantage as the bones are then easily removed when the parcel is opened. My inspiration for this trout dish was one summer whilst planning the television programme HomeGrown. As I sat in the garden the tall fronds of herb fennel were billowing in the sea breeze and I just knew they would blend well with butter and lemon for this delicate fish.

Method

Finely chop the fennel and mix with the butter. Zest the lemon into the butter and season with the salt and pepper. Divide the butter in four and stuff each trout with the herb butter. Place each trout onto a sheet of baking parchment and squeeze the lemon over each fish. Season with a little more salt and pepper. Wrap up the fish using the paper to make a parcel. Secure it so that the steam will not escape during the cooking. This then holds in all the lovely herby butter which bastes the fish.

Place them on a baking sheet and bake in a preheated oven Gas 6/200°C/400°F for 10 to 15 minutes. (The eye of the fish will have turned quite white and bulge a little, showing that the fish is cooked.)

Serve one parcel per person and open them at the table to savour the fennel and lemon aroma. Remove the head and the skin, which should come away easily with the paper, and the fish flesh will fall off the bones into the herb butter.

I like to serve this with stir-fried summer vegetables and new potatoes.

Main Course

50g / 2 oz butter

1 large onion, finely chopped

1 clove garlic

120ml / 4 fl oz dry white wine/stock/water

900ml / 2 pints hot stock (vegetable or fish)

250g / 8 oz arborio rice

more butter

lots of fresh parsley and chives

1 lemon

500g / 1 lb Solway brown shrimps

Shrimp And Herb Risotto

Risotto is the sort of dish that is easy to make at short notice. Arborio rice is the traditional Italian short-grained rice that cooks creamily in 20 minutes. Solway Brown Shrimps give colour and a taste of the sea and sit well with various herbs in season.

Method

Melt the 50g butter in a pan and add the onion, and let this soften for 5 to 10 minutes until the onion is lightly browned. Add the garlic and continue to cook slowly for another 5 minutes. Add the rice and turn it over until all the grains are coated in the oniony butter. Pour in the wine and bring to a simmer, stir well. Heat the stock in another saucepan near by and ladle a little at a time into the rice pan, stirring well until it has all been absorbed before adding more. Continue cooking gently like this until all the stock is used and the rice is tender and creamy but is still whole.

Stir in the shrimps and a little more butter with the freshly chopped herbs and a squeeze of lemon to taste. Serve in individual bowls with more herbs and shrimps to garnish.

Main Course

Herb Filled Carrot Roulade

450g / 1 lb finely grated carrots

50g / 2 oz salted butter

1 teaspoon ground cumin

6 free range eggs, separated

1 x 200g tub cream cheese

fresh herbs – chives and/or parsley finely chopped

salt and pepper

Carrot Roulade has become one of my signature dishes. Make it the day before for convenience and serve it cold as an unusual vegetarian main course. You'll find that the meat eaters will want some too!

Method

Line a swiss roll tin with baking parchment or a non stick-baking sheet. Melt the butter in a saucepan and add the ground cumin. Cook the carrots gently in this mixture for 5 minutes. Season with salt and pepper and cool the mix. Add the egg yolks stirring them well in.

Whisk the egg whites until they form soft peaks then carefully fold in the carrot mixture, taking care to mix one tablespoon at a time, using a figure of 8 movement. Don't be heavy handed at this stage as you could break down the air that you've trapped in the whites. Spread this evenly in the prepared tins and bake at Gas 6/ 200ºC/400°F for 10-15 minutes until firm, golden and risen. Turn out the roulade onto an ironed tea towel on a baking sheet. Cover with another tea towel and leave to cool.

Prepare the filling by beating the cream cheese with the fresh herbs and a little seasoning. Add a tablespoon of milk if this is too thick.

Remove the top cloth and spread the filling over the base. Roll the roulade lifting up the short side of the tea towel to roll the egg mixture. Transfer the roulade to a serving plate making sure that the join is underneath. You can manhandle the roulade quite successfully so don't be scared of it!

Serve slices with salad leaves and a garnish of fresh herbs.

2 tablespoons butter

thumbnail-sized piece fresh ginger, peeled and chopped

2 garlic cloves, chopped

1 tablespoon green peppercorns

1 fresh chilli, deseeded

1 stalk lemon grass, finely chopped

1 lime, juice of

2 tablespoons vegetable stock or water

1 tablespoon ground coriander

coconut milk (either 2"creamed block or 200ml tin)

1 tablespoon peanut butter

1kg / 2 lbs total of onion, carrots, courgette or other vegetables in season

3 tablespoons sunflower oil

2 tablespoons fresh coriander, chopped

salt and pepper to taste

Thai Spiced Vegetables

It was a great surprise to find an old bath inside a polytunnel at Howbarrow Farm growing lemon grass. In fact it's very easy to grow and I've even had a go myself. Lemon grass is much better used fresh and I would tend to shy away from anything that's been tinned or preserved with chemicals – the flavour is never the same (neither is the texture). If you do find a fresh source, buy plenty and freeze it. Coriander is very easy to grow but make sure you buy the variety that keeps its leaf, rather than the one that turns into flowers, and water it well.

Method

Melt the butter and sauté the ginger, garlic, peppercorns, lemon grass and chilli for 2 minutes. Add a little stock or water, peanut butter and lime juice whilst stirring. Gradually add the coconut milk whilst bringing gently to boiling point, reduce the heat and simmer for 10 minutes. Cool slightly then puree in a blender.

Roast the vegetables in sunflower oil and salt and pepper for at least 25 minutes till softened and just turning brown at the edges.

Stir fresh chopped coriander into the sauce, season to taste and pour over the roasted vegetables.

Potato Pancake With Juniper Berries

1kg (2 lbs) starchy old potatoes, well scrubbed

1 tablespoon (10ml) olive oil

1 tablespoon butter

1 teaspoon juniper berries, crushed

salt and freshly ground black pepper to taste

Juniper berries are a good herb to use with both potatoes and venison. Grating old potatoes means that they cook quickly. To stop butter burning use equal quantities of olive oil in the pan.

Method

Coarsely grate the potatoes leaving the skin on, wash under several changes of cold water and drain well. Heat the oil and butter together in a large heavy-based frying pan and place the juniper in this. Stir and immediately add the potatoes, turning them over and over and season them with the salt and black pepper. Softly fold this together and continue to cook until the potatoes are tender and take on a golden hue.

To serve, flatten the dish slightly, transfer to a serving dish and lay venison steaks on top.

Vegetables

Pan-fried Potatoes And Thyme

450g / 1 lb new potatoes – Cara or Charlotte

1 onion, thinly sliced

2 rashers Cumbrian smoked home cured streaky bacon

2 tablespoons olive oil

50g / 2 oz butter

2 cloves garlic, sliced

fresh thyme leaves

This potato dish could be a meal on its own. It has smoked bacon, onions, potatoes and herbs, loads of flavour and a texture of crispy bottom and soft top – it only needs a glass of red wine to be complete. If you want to spend less time cooking then parboil the potato slices, but remember that the slower the cooking the better the flavour.

Method

Slice the washed potatoes into the size of a pound coin. Slice the bacon and fry it in the oil and butter in a large shallow pan until starting to crisp. Add the onion and cook until it is soft and pale gold. Add the potatoes and season well with salt, pepper, garlic and thyme. Stir the mixture well to cover each potato slice with the onion and bacon. Turn the heat down as low as possible and cover the pan. Stir from time to time. After 40 minutes the potatoes should be cooked. They sometimes start to burn at the base of the pan, which makes the finished dish lovely and crisp. Serve straight from the pan.

vegetables

1kg / 2 lbs old potatoes

milk and butter to mash

2 teaspoons freshly grated nutmeg

salt and pepper

3 large onions

2 tablespoons each of butter and olive oil

1 x 142 ml pot sour cream

lots of fresh parsley

Cream Topped Mashed Potatoes

My son Alex had been living in Lithuania and I was inspired to make this simple but flavoursome potato dish after a visit there. You could make it one day in advance and do the final cooking when needed the next day. I love the crispy onions intermingled with the nutmegy mash and sour cream. Perfect comfort food in wintertime.

Method

When cooking old potatoes, place them cut in large chunks in the saucepan with just enough water to cover them. Add a teaspoon of salt and put on the lid. Bring the pan to the boil, let it roll for about one minute and turn the heat source off. The potatoes should then cook evenly and not go into a mush. Take a peek in the pan and test them from time to time.

Cook the potatoes in boiling water on a low heat so that they don't disintegrate or as above. Drain and mash using as much milk and butter to create a creamy purée, seasoning with the grated nutmeg.

Whilst the potatoes are cooking, finely slice the onions and cook in a mixture of butter and olive oil so that they are golden and starting to crisp (see photograph). This may take 30 minutes. Season with salt and black pepper.

Starting with the potatoes, spread a layer on the bottom of the baking dish and continue layering with the onions until both have been used up, finishing with the onions. Spread the sour cream on top of the vegetables and bake in the centre of a preheated moderate oven Gas 4/180°C/350°F for 20 minutes until thoroughly heated and the cream has started to brown.

Vegetables

1kg / 2 lb fresh spinach
leaves

50g / 2 oz butter

half a nutmeg, grated

Buttered Spinach

If you have spinach in the garden you'll know how easy it is to grow. I plant several kinds of green leafy plants including spinach, Swiss Chard (a variety called Bright Lights is particularly attractive) and kale. Perpetual spinach is useful as it dies back a little in the winter (depending on the severity of the cold) and re-emerges in the springtime. One of the drawbacks however is that you do need lots of leaves to make a decent portion.

These plants can all be grown in an ornamental garden to mix in with the flowers.

Method

Wash the leaves and place them in a saucepan. Add no water but cook the leaves over a low heat in their own liquid with the lid on. Shake the pan from time to time and peek in the pan to check that the leaves have fallen to the bottom. Remove the pan from the heat and squeeze out all possible juices which can be kept to add to a soup. Chop the spinach finely.

Melt the butter in the pan, add the grated nutmeg and return the spinach to the pan to reheat. Serve as a rich side vegetable with chicken or fish.

50g / 2 oz butter

1 tablespoon olive oil

2 tablespoons light muscovado sugar

4 tablespoons Cumberland raspberry vinegar

900g / 2 lbs baby onions, peeled and trimmed

2 bay leaves and 4 sprigs of fresh thyme

45g / 3 tablespoons raisins

45g / 3 tablespoons pine nuts

Sweet & Sour Onions

This is one of my favourite ways of using onions. If you have a glut of shallots or even large onions which can be cut in quarters leaving the root end on, I encourage you to make this. Serve it with plain grilled chicken or duck breast. It freezes quite well too.

Method

Melt the butter with the oil in a large ovenproof dish or pan. Add the muscovado and half the vinegar, then tip in the onions (they should be in one layer) and stir to coat them in the hot butter.

Scatter over the bay leaves and thyme. Cook over a medium heat for 20 minutes without stirring.

Preheat the oven to Gas 2/150°C/300°F.

Give the onions a good stir. Add the raisins, pine nuts, the rest of the vinegar plus 1 tablespoon water and season with salt and pepper. Bake in the oven for 45 minutes until the onions are caramelised. Serve warm.

Vegetables

Braised Shallots

1kg / 2 lbs shallots

100g / 4 oz butter

vegetable or chicken stock

fresh thyme

2 cloves garlic

1 dessertspoon coriander seeds, slightly crushed

lots of fresh coriander leaves or parsley to garnish

salt and pepper

Parboiling shallots starts the cooking process for these braised shallots. This dish freezes well and it's worth making double, one to eat and one to freeze.

Method

Peel the shallots and place in a pan of boiling water for 4 minutes. Remove and put to one side.

In a large oven-proof casserole melt the butter without colouring. Roll the shallots in the butter until well covered. Pour in stock to come halfway up the shallots. Add a sprig of thyme, the crushed garlic and coriander seeds with the seasoning.

Cover the pot and put over a low heat in the oven until the shallots are just cooked (the time will depend on the size of the shallots). The liquid can be evaporated off. Serve with fresh coriander or parsley sprinkled over the top.

1 tablespoon olive oil

1 onion

3 leeks, washed and cut on the diagonal

3 Jerusalem artichokes, well scrubbed

3 carrots, scrubbed

Stir-fry Winter Vegetables

If you don't have a wok use a heavy based frying pan: one with deep sides is best. Get the pan very hot and keep it hot without burning to cook the vegetables crisply. Turn them often.

I grow Jerusalem artichokes as a screen in the summer (they are related to the sunflower and can grow to over six feet high) and are a useful root vegetable in the winter. They have a smoky flavour and give a crunch to the other vegetables.

Method

Prepare the vegetables by washing the leeks under a cold tap to get rid of all the soil and slice thinly. Peel the onion and slice it finely. Scrub the carrots and cut in thin slivers with the potato peeler. Slice the Jerusalem artichokes thickly.

Heat the oil in a wok or large frying pan and stir-fry the onion slices until they start to turn golden. Add the leeks, carrots and artichokes and continue to stir-fry for about 3 minutes. Season with salt and freshly ground black pepper. Add one tablespoon of hot water and cover the pan to allow the vegetables to steam cook. Remove the lid, stir well to evaporate the liquid and place in a serving dish.

Vegetables

4 Pak Choi plants

2 tablespoons sesame seeds

2 tablespoons sunflower oil

1 tablespoon sesame oil

1 piece of fresh ginger (thumbnail size)

2 spring onions, finely sliced diagonally

Steamed Chinese Leaves

At one time we were only able to buy one sort of Chinese leaf in our shops, but many different types are now available for buying and growing. Choose one of the deeper coloured leaves to grow, plant them either early in the season or late and keep them well watered as they tend to go to seed very quickly.

Method

Wash the Pak Choi and keep it whole. Steam it for no longer than 5 minutes. Put on a warmed serving dish to keep warm.

Dry fry the sesame seeds in a pan until golden - watch them jump! Put them to one side. Add the sunflower and sesame oils to a small pan and heat slowly. Grate the ginger and add to the pan. Keep the heat low.

Pour the heated oil over the Pak Choi and garnish with the spring onions and sesame seeds.

Beetroot With Apple And Horseradish Cream

2 medium sized beetroots, cooked and peeled

2 dessert apples

1 tablespoon sunflower oil

25g/1 oz butter

2 tablespoons lemon juice

1/2 teaspoon creamed horseradish

fresh parsley, finely chopped

Beetroot can be used in so many recipes and is underrated in my eyes. It's a sweet root suitable for soups, roasting, boiling and eating cold – but not with vinegar. Ugh!

However my neighbour Chris does make a great beetroot jelly. Here I've combined two autumn ingredients and served them hot.

Dice the cooked beetroots and place in an ovenproof serving dish. Keep this warm whilst preparing the apples. Heat the oil and butter in a pan and lightly cook the chunks of apple until just starting to turn golden. Lay these on top of the beetroot and keep them warm. Add the lemon juice and creamed horseradish to the pan with a tablespoon or two of water to deglaze the pan. Pour this over the beetroot and apple and serve with a sprinkling of fresh herbs.

Puddings & Cakes

I suppose I should apologise for putting in three chocolate recipes here but, well - chocolate's good. It's perhaps worth remembering how nutritious it is! It sits along beautifully with fruit in most seasons. I try to buy 'fairly traded' cocoa and coffee as they are products that can really make a difference to the farmers in developing countries.

50g / 2 oz self-raising 85% flour

75g / 3 oz caster sugar

25g / 1 oz organic cocoa

1 teaspoon baking powder

25g / 1 oz well softened butter

75g / 3 oz eggs (weighed shell on)

100g / 4 oz cleaned soft fruit raspberries/strawberries

500ml / 1 lb tub of your favourite vanilla ice cream

2 egg whites

100g / 4 oz white caster sugar

Chocolate Baked Alaska

I like to make this update of the Baked Alaska in summertime when the soft fruits become available. Strawberries and chocolate are a marvellous combination, but then so are chocolate with raspberries, blackberries, cherries, apples, pears and damsons. This is a very simple all in one recipe that requires the butter to be really soft so that the mix combines easily.

Method

Prepare a flan tin by lining with baking parchment. Preheat the oven to Gas 3/170ºC/325°F.

Crack the eggs into a bowl and mix all the other ingredients together for at least one minute. Place in the prepared flan tin and bake in the preheated oven for 30 minutes until risen and set.

Turn out and cool.

Place the sponge on a cold baking sheet and scatter the berries on top. Use the ice cream to cover the fruit and place the dish in the freezer.

Make a meringue by whisking the 2 egg whites until stiff in a large clean bowl and gradually whisk in 4 oz (100g) white caster sugar. Cover the ice cream and sponge completely with the meringue and return this to the freezer for at least one hour.

Bake at Gas 9/ 240˚C/475°F in the middle of the oven for 5 to 10 minutes until golden brown. Be careful it doesn't burn and be prepared to watch it in the oven and turn it at least once.

Serve immediately.

65g /2½ oz organic cocoa powder

275g / 10 oz self-raising flour

pinch salt

220g /7½ oz caster sugar

300ml / ½ pint sunflower oil

1 teaspoon vanilla extract

3 free range eggs, beaten

250g / 9oz cooked beetroot, grated

Chocolate Beetroot Cake

This cake came as a bit of a surprise but considering we use carrots in a cake, why not beetroots? They give a sweet moistness to the cake as well as a deepening of colour.

Method

Sift the cocoa and flour with the salt and the sugar.

Whisk the sunflower oil, vanilla and eggs together until thick (this may take a good 5 minutes of whisking), add the beetroot and mix well with the dry ingredients until it is a glorious purple colour.

Pour into a prepared 2 x 18cm (7") sandwich tins and bake in a preheated oven Gas 5/190°C/375°F for about 35 minutes or until the cake springs back when pressed lightly in the middle.

Allow to cool slightly before removing from the cake tin.

Make a chocolate ganache (see below) to fill the cooled cake.

150g / 5 oz dark chocolate

150ml / ¼ pint double cream

900g / 2 lbs ripe but firm pears

1 free range egg

1 cinnamon stick

175g / 6 oz sugar

2 dessertspoons organic cocoa

75g / 3 oz self-raising flour

3 tablespoons butter, melted

½ teaspoon vanilla essence

Ganache

Chop the chocolate roughly on a clean dry board and transfer it to a mixing bowl.

In a saucepan heat the cream until just below boiling and pour this over the chocolate. Stir gently until the chocolate melts and both are well blended. Whisk the mixture until it is fluffy and cool. It will go quite thick. Use this to sandwich together the two halves of the cake. Dust with icing sugar and decorate with marzipan beetroots.

Chocolate Pear Pudding

There's something very comforting about making this Chocolate Pear Pudding in the autumn.

If you have too many ripe pears then use them but omit the first cooking as they will soften considerably in the oven.

Method

Cook the pears in a saucepan with a little water and the cinnamon stick and half the sugar.

Drain the pears and keep the juice. Place the pears in a large buttered ovenproof dish.

Mix together the sugar and half the cocoa and sprinkle this over the pears. Moisten the dish with a few tablespoons of the pear juice and drink the rest.

Beat the egg with the remaining sugar until it thickens and turns a lighter colour. Add the melted butter and mix well. Sieve the flour and remaining cocoa together and fold this into the egg mixture with the vanilla essence. Spread this over the pears and place the dish on a baking sheet to prevent spillage. Bake in a preheated oven Gas 6/ 200°C/400°F for about 25 minutes until the top is set.

Puddings & Cakes

568ml / 1 pint full fat whole milk

25g / 1 oz butter

grated rind of 1 large unwaxed lemon

2 large free range eggs

175g / 6 oz caster sugar

100g / 3½ oz fine fresh breadcrumbs

2 level tablespoons blackcurrant or other dark, fruity jam

Queen Of Puddings

My Mum used to make us a Queen of Puddings on a Sunday and we children thought of it as a rare and expensive treat. Little did we know that it's a cheap and cheerful way of making a little go a long way, often using up stale bread and the last of a pot of jam. This recipe however takes it one stage further using proper milk and lemon and a good dark jam to act as a striking layer between the eggy base and the crisp meringue topping.

Method

Put the milk, butter and lemon rind in a pan and heat gently until the butter melts. Set to one side until lukewarm. Mix the egg yolks and 1 oz (25g) of the sugar together in a bowl until thoroughly combined and then blend in the warm milk. Add the breadcrumbs and pour into a 2 pint ovenproof dish. Leave to stand for 20 minutes.

Put the dish in a roasting tin with enough hot water to come halfway up the sides. Cook at Gas 4/180°C/350°F for 25 to 30 minutes or until just set in the centre. Allow this to cool for about 20 minutes. Spread the jam over the top of the custard.

Whisk the egg whites to a stiff peak and then whisk in the remaining sugar a spoonful at a time until stiff and glossy. Spoon this meringue on top of the jam and bake at Gas 3/170°C/325°F for 10 to 15 minutes or until the top is golden and crisp.

Serve warm with cream.

Rich Shortcrust Pastry

225g/8 oz plain flour, sieved

175g/6 oz butter, cold from the fridge

1 egg yolk

2-3 tablespoons water

My Mum makes the best pastry (and the best Yorkshire Puds too, but that's another story). She's had 80 years of making it, so she should be good by now! It is said that you need cool, light hands to get the best result. You can always use a mixer on its lowest speed to save your arms, but honestly it's a great feeling getting your hands in! Don't knead pastry, bind it together gently with your fingers.

Method

To keep the pastry short and light, sieve the flour and use the butter straight from the fridge, cutting it in with a rounded end knife. And butter is the only fat that gives wonderful flavour to shortcrust pastry so don't stint by using other processed fat.

In a large bowl rub the butter into the flour using your fingertips until an even mix of crumbs is made. Mix the yolk and water together and pour this in slowly to bind the pastry using your hands or a knife until a soft smooth dough is formed. Leave this to relax for about 20 minutes in a cool place.

Cumberland Rum Nicky

350g / 12 oz rich shortcrust pastry (see previous recipe)

50g / 2 oz preserved ginger (in syrup), or pear and ginger jam

1 tablespoon caster sugar

100g / 4 oz chopped dates

50g / 2 oz butter

2 tablespoons rum

Cumberland Rum Nicky is an old recipe that crops up in lots of different forms. It uses rich spicy ginger with dates and rum – all ingredients that would have been imported into the county at Whitehaven 200 years ago. I like to make this at Christmas time with the seasonal garnish of trees.

Method

Line a buttered pie plate with two thirds of the pastry and cover with the chopped dates and sliced ginger or pear and ginger jam. Beat the butter, sugar and rum together and pour this over the dates.

Cover with the remaining pastry, either in lattice work or for Christmas with holly leaf or tree shapes. Use an egg wash to brush over the pastry and bake in a preheated moderately hot oven at Gas 6/200°C/400°F for 10 to 15 minutes. Turn the heat down to Gas 4/180°C/350°F and bake for another 30 minutes until the pastry is golden.

Serve with cream or Cumberland Rum Butter.

Puddings & Cakes

Rosemary And Lemon Cake

4 tablespoons zest and juice from 1 unwaxed lemon

1 tablespoon finely chopped rosemary

225g / 8 oz unsalted butter, softened

175g / 6 oz light caster sugar

2 free range eggs, beaten

350g / 12 oz plain flour

2 level teaspoons baking powder

1-2 tablespoons milk (or buttermilk)

1 level tablespoon caster sugar

Rosemary is in season all the year round. You can use it for both savoury and sweet dishes and even the flowers are edible. I always think it's worth making double of this mix and freezing one of the finished cakes.

Method

Prepare a 2 lb (900g) loaf tin. Preheat the oven to Gas 3/170°C/325°F.

Place the softened butter, sugar, lemon zest and rosemary in a mixing bowl and whisk until light and fluffy. Gradually whisk in the beaten eggs, adding a little of the flour if the mixture looks as if it might curdle.

Fold in the rest of the sifted flour and baking powder and a pinch of salt. Stir in the lemon juice. The mixture should have a soft dropping consistency; if it is a bit stiff stir in one or two tablespoons of milk.

Place the mix into the prepared loaf tin, level the surface and sprinkle with the tablespoon of caster sugar. Bake in the preheated oven for one hour. The cake may take slightly longer to cook, depending on your oven. Test with a clean skewer that it comes out clean. Cool in the tin for 10 minutes before turning out and cool completely on a wire rack. Wrap in foil to keep the cake.

200g / 7 oz 85% flour from The Watermill

50g / 2 oz raw cane light brown sugar

pinch salt

100g / 3½ oz butter

1 teaspoon lemon juice

700g / 1½ lbs rhubarb, peeled and cut into small pieces

150g / 6 oz sugar

3 free range eggs

750g curd or cream cheese

1 orange - zest and juice

1 teaspoon vanilla extract

1 teaspoon cornflour

Rhubarb Cheesecake

My friend in Germany inspired this pudding for making in the spring when the first rhubarb looks like sparkling jewels sitting under the creamy topping. The combination of orange and rhubarb is always good.

Method

Rub the butter into the flour with the salt. Add 50g / 2oz light brown sugar and moisten with the lemon juice to form a dough. Knead lightly and cover with cling film and leave in the fridge for at least 30 minutes to relax. Roll this into the base of a 26cm cake tin with a loose bottom lined with baking sheet or parchment. Bake in a preheated hot oven for 10 minutes. Place the rhubarb on top. Beat the sugar and eggs until creamy and add the soft cheese. Zest the orange and add with the juice mixed with the cornflour. Whisk all well. Pour this on top of the rhubarb. Bake in a preheated oven Gas 2/150°C/300°F for 1 hour, then leave it in the oven to cool down.

This is often better made the day before and kept in the fridge overnight to set. Remove from the fridge for at least half an hour before serving to bring back to room temperature.

4 large baking apples

25g/1 oz butter

4 teaspoons demerara sugar

50g/2 oz dried fruit – dates, raisins, sultanas, cherries

1 tablespoon chopped hazelnuts/toasted almonds

Baked Apples

Dave Drewery the potter from Appleby makes lovely apple bakers. These are ideal for making individual baked apples (or pears) that can be left in the oven until needed. Use a variety of apple that cooks to a fluff such as Bramleys or Codlings. The resulting pudding will have its own sweet sauce in the bottom of each dish.

Method

Wash the apples, core them and with a sharp knife cut around the 'waist' of each fruit.

Smear the butter on the bottom of each apple baker. Place one apple in each dish.

In a small bowl, mix the sugar, dried fruit and chopped hazelnuts.

With a teaspoon, stuff this mixture into the centre hole of each apple.

It doesn't matter if this tumbles into the dish too. Pour a tablespoon of hot water into the base of each baker and this will make the lovely syrup. Put the lid on each apple baker. Place the dishes into a preheated medium oven for 25 minutes or until the fruits are browned and cooked through.

Serve with thick double cream or yogurt.

Hazelnut Meringues With Fresh Raspberry Cream

weight of 2 egg whites

double their weight in raw cane caster sugar (break down any lumps you may find)

50g / 2 oz hazelnuts, plus some extra to decorate the finished meringues

300ml / ½ pint double cream

2 dessertspoonfuls fresh or frozen raspberries, drained

Meringues are easy to make; just make sure that all your utensils, bowls and whisks have no trace of grease on them or the whites won't hold the air and go stiff.

If there are ever any egg whites left over from a recipe I freeze them. When I need to use them they are thawed to room temperature and then weighed so that I can calculate double their weight in raw cane caster sugar. Using this type of brown sugar gives a good caramelised taste to the meringues.

One summer, years ago, I tasted a superb raspberry cream cake and was inspired to use the cream with meringues. I used the technique of pushing fresh raspberries through whipped double cream and it worked!

Method

Pre heat the oven to Gas 1/4/100°C/200°F.

To toast the hazelnuts, place them on a baking sheet under a preheated grill and grill them until they are browned all over. Be careful to watch them as this process won't take long and they may burn. When they are cold rub the skins from the nuts and crush with a rolling pin or whiz up in a nut mill.

Make sure the bowl and whisk are completely clean and dry, as any sign of grease will stop the whites from whipping up.

Using a machine, whisk the egg whites until they are stiff. Gradually add spoonfuls of the lump-free caster sugar whilst whisking continuously. The mixture will become smooth and close and will stand in stiff peaks. Fold in the remaining sugar using a large metal spoon. Fold in the crushed hazelnuts.

Have ready a flat baking tin lined with a non-stick baking sheet. Using two spoons, one filled with the mixture, take the empty spoon and place it under the mixture to push the meringue on to the baking sheet. This should make egg shaped mounds: try and get an even number so that they can be sandwiched together. Place the tins in the oven and leave until the meringues are completely dried out.

Mix the whipped cream with the raspberries until the cream turns pink, leaving some fruits whole.

When the meringues are cooked and completely cold, sandwich two of them together with the raspberry cream and decorate with fresh raspberries and hazelnuts. Delicious!

Puddings & Cakes

250g/8 oz self raising flour

1 tablespoon raw cane caster sugar

1 teaspoon baking powder

50g/2 oz butter at room temperature

about1/4 pint natural yogurt

Scones

Traditional scones for jam and cream are easy to make but are better when made with a light hand. Don't be too rough once the dough has been formed. When cutting try and stamp them out using the cutter straight up and down, rather than pulling to one side as this could lead to leaning towers of scones. But don't worry they will taste just as good. If you are able to get fresh buttermilk, then use it, otherwise the best quality natural yogurt is fine. Scones will last longer using buttermilk or yogurt. Scones will freeze very well and only need a warm oven to refresh them once they're thawed.

Method

Sift together the dry ingredients and cut the butter into this. Rub the butter in until it resembles fine breadcrumbs. Gradually mix in the natural yogurt until a soft dough is formed. Turn the dough onto a floured board and press down gently. Lightly roll or use your fingers to produce a round about 3/4" thick. Using a cutter stamp out the scones and place on a baking sheet. Brush the tops with milk.

Bake in a preheated oven at No. 7, 210ºC, 425ºF, for about 10 minutes. Cool completely and eat with fresh whipped cream and your favourite jam.

450g / 1 lb ripe elderberries

450g / 1 lb ripe cooking apples

150ml / ¼ pint water

900g / 2 lb sugar

Grandma's Elderberry And Apple Jam

I have had to amend my Grandma's original handwritten recipe to include metric equivalent weights and details on the setting. The recipe that I found was all of four lines but I see that I've made a note underneath that it was easy to make, the colour and flavour were outstanding.

Method

Remove and clean the elderberries from their stalks.

Wash, core and chop the apples.

Put the sugar to warm in a big bowl in a slow oven. Prepare the jars by washing thoroughly and place them in the oven to sterilize them.

Place the prepared fruits in a large jam pan or similar, with the water.

Bring this to the boil and simmer the fruit until it is all tender.

Add the warmed sugar and stir well to help it to dissolve.

Bring this back to the boil and continue to cook until a 'set' is reached. Use a jam thermometer to register 220°F for a set.

Turn off the heat and leave for about 15 minutes to cool slightly, then pour the hot jam into the hot jars and place the lids on immediately. Make sure the lids are on securely and turn the jars upside down to create a vacuum. Leave the jars to cool then label each one.

Bread

Making bread is great therapy. When I taught special needs students at the college in Carlisle I always made bread in the first lesson. There's something about getting the hands into a dough that's warm and soft and being able to move it about roughly without harming it. Making pastry requires cool light hands; breadmaking requires a bit of effort, but that's all, anyone can make bread.

It isn't quite so important to be accurate when weighing out ingredients for bread making so if the dough appears too wet more flour can be added, though I should add here that a wet dough is preferable to a dry one for a lighter, moist crusty loaf.

Using a reliable yeast is important and that's why I tend to use Fermipan which is available at most health food stores. Any other dried yeast that suits you is fine, and if you have a reliable source of fresh yeast then so much the better. I often say that bread has a mind of its own and its rising qualities are affected by the mood you're in, the weather, the ambience of the room, and even the price of bacon!

Please don't be put off, do give it a try - bread making is a simple, though slightly time consuming process that is so rewarding when it comes out of the oven perfuming the whole kitchen and making it hard to resist. If you start the mix off last thing at night and place the dough (covered) in the fridge, you can continue cooking it next morning and it will have been proving while you've been asleep.

And if you have a bread maker, well, that's fine too! At least you have control over what the ingredients are in your own home baked loaf.

If your cooking time is up but the bread doesn't come out of the tin easily, leave it another 10 minutes and it will be cooked through.

500g/1 lb organic strong white flour

1 tablespoon Fermipan yeast or other dried yeast

1 teaspoon salt

6 tablespoons extra virgin olive oil

coarse sea salt

3 large tomatoes

2 tablespoons fresh herbs in season (parsley, chives, fennel, etc)

2 cloves fresh garlic

Flat Bread With Tomatoes And Garlic

I first saw this bread at a village bakery in Menorca and was determined to try it back home in Cumbria. When tomatoes are plentiful and full of ripe flavour this is a bread that can be eaten with a crisp salad for lunch. This recipe is suitable for vegans and it can be frozen.

Method

Put the flour and Fermipan in a bowl with the fine salt and pour in about 4 tablespoons of the oil. Mix very quickly and then gradually add about 300ml (1/2pint) warm water to form a soft dough. Mix again and then knead quickly on the table. Return the dough to the bowl and cover. Leave in a warm place until doubled in size.

Knock the dough back and press it out or roll it in an even layer on a non-stick baking sheet. Cut the tomatoes into thick slices and place on the risen dough. Brush the top of the dough with the remaining oil. In a small bowl, mix the fresh herbs and crushed garlic with a grinding of sea salt and black pepper and sprinkle this over each cut tomato. Leave in a warm place until risen again.

Have the oven ready at Gas 7/220°C/425°F and bake the bread until golden. This may take 20 minutes. Eat while still warm.

Onion Caraway Bread

450g/1 lb organic strong white flour from The Watermill

1 tablespoon Fermipan or dried yeast

2 tablespoons extra virgin olive oil

1 teaspoon salt

1 teaspoon caraway seeds

4 medium onions finely sliced

1 teaspoon salt

6 tablespoons olive oil

1 bay leaf

2 teaspoons sugar

1 free range egg

fresh rosemary

lots of freshly ground black pepper

another teaspoon caraway seed

This has become one of my favourite breads to make and eat! I think the secret of it is the sweetness of the onions marrying with the freshly ground black pepper which is essential at the end of the cooking. Caraway is a seed that's gone out of fashion in this country, so let's enjoy it in this bread.

Method

Prepare the bread dough by mixing the flour, Fermipan and olive oil with one teaspoon of caraway seeds and salt. Add sufficient warm water to bind it all together. Knead by hand until the dough is smooth and elastic. Leave it to prove covered in a warm place until it has doubled or tripled in size.

Whilst the dough is rising, heat the 6 tablespoons olive oil and soften the sliced onions very slowly without colouring them. Add the sugar, salt and bay leaf and rosemary. Continue to cook slowly. Cool.

When this has cooled, beat the egg and add to the mixture. Add the caraway seeds and stir to blend (the caraway would become bitter if cooked for too long).

Knock back the raised dough and shape into a rectangle. Roll this into the shape of a large swiss roll tin which has been previously lined with a non-stick baking sheet. Press the dough to fit the tin. Spread the onion mixture evenly on the bread dough, going right up to the edge. Place in the centre of the preheated oven Gas 8/ 230ºC/450ºF to cook for about 25 minutes. Remove from the oven and sprinkle generously with black pepper. Use scissors to cut this delicious bread and serve in little squares as an appetiser or in larger wedges with a tossed green salad for a light lunch.

350g / 12 oz wholewheat self-raising flour

1 tablespoon sugar

½ tsp salt (optional)

150ml / ½ pt Yates bitter beer

50g / 2 oz butter, melted

Beer Bread Mini Loaves

Children are often enticed to make little loaves and the sooner we encourage our children to enjoy cooking, the sooner their diets should improve. These loaves are made with self-raising flour and require no yeast and are very quick to make.

Method

Preheat oven to Gas 7/220°C/425°F. Grease six one-cup/mini loaf tins. In a large bowl, combine flour, sugar, and salt. Add beer and butter; stir just until combined – it should be a sloppy mixture. Spoon it evenly into the prepared pans and place in the oven. Bake for 20-35 minutes, until the edges are golden. Remove from the tins, return to the oven to crisp the bottoms and cool on a wire rack. Makes 6 loaves.

Birdoswald Cheese Bread

125g / 4 oz Birdoswald cheese or similar cut into dice

1 tablespoon Fermipan or similar instant yeast

225g / 8 oz wholewheat flour

225g / 8 oz strong white flour

1 teaspoon salt

175ml / 6 fl oz natural yogurt

75ml / 3 fl oz hot water

An excellent bread for salad sandwiches or beans on toast! Once the bread is cooked the lumps of cheese sit enticingly in each slice.

Method

In a large mixing bowl place the flours and salt, mix well and add the Fermipan. Mix the yogurt with the hot water to take the chill from it, and add this to the flour. Mix all together to form a soft dough and then knead well.

Leave the dough to rise in a warm place, covered, for about 45 minutes until doubled in size.

Knock back the dough and divide it in half. Form two balls and flatten the dough slightly. Scatter the cheese over the bread and press it into the dough. Shape to fit the loaf tins which have been greased. Place in the tins and cover again and leave in a moist place for 10 minutes.

Bake in a hot oven, Gas 7/220°C/425°F, for about 25 minutes.

The cheese may stick to the tin, so run a knife around the edge carefully before removing from the tin.

I did leave this loaf in the oven rather longer than necessary as you can see by the dark crust! It was still delicious.

Bread

Buttermilk Bread Sticks

1 tablespoon Fermipan yeast or other dried quick-action yeast

285ml / ½ pint Cream of Cumbria Buttermilk

450g / 1 lb Watermill organic strong white bread flour

1 teaspoon salt

beaten egg to glaze

poppy seeds to glaze

This bread has a moist centre and crispy crust. If you are unable to get real buttermilk, use natural yogurt instead.

Method

Take the buttermilk from the fridge 20 minutes before starting to make the bread in order to bring it to room temperature.

Place the flour in a mixing bowl and stir in the salt. Mix in the Fermipan yeast and add the buttermilk and enough warm water to make a soft dough. Place the dough on a floured work surface and knead for a few minutes until the dough is smooth. Leave to rise in a warm place covered with a warm, damp tea towel. Knock back, punching the dough to remove the bubbles that have been formed during rising. Shape the dough into long sausages. Grease French bread tins and place the dough in the tins.

Brush with the beaten egg to glaze the bread and sprinkle with the seeds.

Keep in a moist, warm place for 10 minutes and then put into a preheated hot oven with plenty of water sprayed over the loaves. Bake at Gas 7/220°C/425°F for 20 minutes until the loaves are golden and crisp. Remove from the tin and lower the heat for a further 5 minutes. Cool, uncovered on a wire rack.

(If you don't have French bread tins, place the sausage shapes on a heated baking tray which has been dusted with flour, use the beaten egg to glaze the bread and scatter the seeds on top. Place this directly into the hot oven. This means that the bread cooks quickly and keeps its shape without the second rising.)

Bread

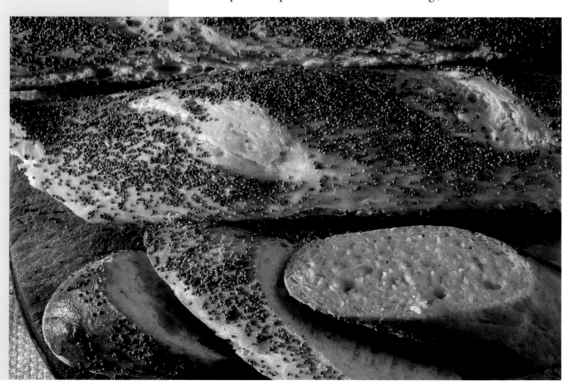

450g / 14 oz Miller's Magic flour

1 tablespoon Fermipan or other instant dried yeast

1 teaspoon salt

2 tablespoons olive oil

275ml / ½ pint warm water

Millers Magic Loaves

Rye flour has long been seen as a difficult flour from which to make a decent loaf. The combination of rye flour and wholemeal makes a really good loaf that does rise.

Method

Place the flour and salt in a large mixing bowl and stir well. Add the Fermipan, stir well and add the olive oil. Pour in the warm water and mix to a soft dough. Remove from the bowl onto a floured work surface and knead it until a smooth dough is formed. Cover this with an upturned bowl and leave it to rise for about one hour.

Remove the bowl, knock back the dough to its original size and shape into a prepared bread tin or straight onto a non-stick baking sheet.

Leave this in a warm place without any draughts for 20 minutes until it has risen again. If you have a top oven or grill area on your cooker, once the oven is on, the heat will rise sufficiently to warm this space for the second rising of the bread.

Place in a preheated oven Gas 7/220°C/425°F for 30 minutes until the loaf comes out of the tin easily.

Bread

Appendix

Where To Buy Cumbrian Food

I would recommend visiting markets in towns throughout the region. As well as local town markets, Farmers' Markets are held regularly at:

Brampton	last Sat	9am-2.30pm	by the Moot Hall
Brough	3rd Sat	9.30am-2(1)pm	in the Memorial Hall
Carlisle	1st Fri	9.30am-3.30pm	in the City Centre
Carnforth	4th Wed	9.30am-2.30pm	in the Railway Station
Egremont	3rd Fri	9am-2.30pm	in the Market Hall
Harrison & Hetherington	2nd Sat	9.30am-1.30pm	Borderway Mart, Rosehill, Carlisle
Kendal	last Fri	9.30am-3.30pm	in the Market Square
Orton	2nd Sat	9.30am-2.30pm	in the Market Hall
Penrith	3rd Tue	9am-2.30pm	in the Market Square
Pooley Bridge	last Sun (Apr-Sep)	10.30am-2.30pm	behind the Sun Inn
Ulverston	3rd Sat	9am-2.30pm	outside the Market Hall
Whitehaven	1st Sat	10am-2.30pm	in Morrisons Car Park

In addition to producers highlighted in the book here is a selection of some other stockists of Cumbrian food. All locations are Cumbria unless otherwise stated.

The Bakehouse
Prince's Street
Broughton in Furness LA20 6HQ
Tel: 01229 716284

Bell's Fishmongers & Licensed Game Dealers Ltd
16 Westmoor Road
Kingstown
Carlisle CA3 OHD
Tel: 01228 542924

Booths Artisan
Wainwrights Yard,
Kendal LA9 4DP,
Tel 01539 723706

Booths
Dogeson Croft Road
Kirkby Londsdale LA6 2HG
Tel: 015242 73443

Booths
Tithebarn Street
Keswick CA12 5EA
Tel: 017687 73518

Booths
The Old Station
Victoria Street
Windermere LA23 1QA
Tel: 015394 46114
www.booths-supermarkets.co.uk

Brunswick Deli
9 Brunswick Rd
Penrith CA11 7LU
Tel: 01768 210500

Cartmel Village Shop
The Square
Cartmel
Grange over Sands LA11 6QB
Tel: 015395 36201

Castletown Farm Shop
Floriston
Rigg
Rockcliffe
Carlisle CA6 4HG
Tel:01228 674400

Churchmouse Cheeses
4 Market St
Kirkby Lonsdale LA6 2 AU
Tel: 015242 73005

Country Cuts Farm Shop
Bridge End Farm
Santon Bridge
Holmrook CA19 IUY
Tel: 01946 726256

Country Markets Limited, Cumberland and West-
morland (these used to be W.I. markets): these are
seasonal markets, usually closed January.
Noreen Woolaghan contact for Cumberland –
01946 823452
Peggy Roberts contact for Westmorland –
015394 32718
Ambleside – Friday, St. John's Ambulance Hall,
Stock Ghyl Lane 10 am -11.30
Brampton – Wednesday, The Moot Hall
8 a.m. to 11.30 a.m.
Cockermouth - Friday, United Reform Church,
Main St., 9 a.m. – 12 noon
Eden Valley – Friday, Appleby Public Hall,
8.30 a.m. – 11 a.m
Kirkby Lonsdale – Thursday, The Institute,
New Road, 10 a.m. – 12 noon
Milnthorpe – Friday, Cross Keys Hotel,
10 a.m. – 11.30 a.m.
Penrith – Friday, St. Andrew's Parish Rooms,
8.30 a.m. – 11.30 a.m.
Ulverston – Thursday, Coronation Hall,
9 a.m. – 11.30 a.m
Whitehaven – Thursday, College Street,
9.30 a.m. – 12 noon
Wigton – Tuesday, Market Hall,
8.30 a.m. – 1 p.m.

Cranstons Food Hall
Ullswater Rd
Penrith CA11 7EH
Tel: 01768 868680

The Farm and Flower Shop,
Orton Grange
Carlisle CA5 6LA
Tel: 01228 711410

J & J Graham Ltd
7 Market Square
Penrith CA10
Tel: 01768 862281

Greystone House Farm Shop
Stainton
Penrith CA11 0EF
Tel: 01768 866952

Half Moon Wholefoods
14 Front Street
Brampton
Cumbria CA8 1NG
Tel: 016977 3775
www.halfmoonwholefoods.co.uk
Email chris@halfmoonwholefoods.co.uk

Holker Food Hall
Holker Hall
Cark-in-Cartmel
Grange-o-Sands
Cumbria LA11 7PL
Tel: 015395 58328l or 59084

Kitridding Farm Shop
Kitridding Farm
Old Town,
Near Kirkby Lonsdale LA6 2QAQ
Tel: 015395 67484

The Laird's Larder
16 Fisher St
Carlisle CA3 8RN
Tel:01228 537769

LOMAS – Fishmonger
4 Wampool Street
SILLOTH
Cumbria   CA7 4AA
Telephone: 016973 31334

Low Sizergh Barn
Sizergh
Kendal LA8 8AE
Tel: 015395 60426

Lucy's Specialist Grocers
Church St
Ambleside LA22 0BU
Tel:015394 32223

Made In Cumbria Shop
Moto Services M6 Motorway
Whitecarr Road, Bay Horse,
Lancashire LA2 9DU
Tel: 01524 792871

Mansergh Hall Farm Shop
Mansergh
Nr. Kirkby Lonsdale LA6 2EN
Tel:015242 71397

Sarah Nelson's Grasmere Gingerbread
Church Cottage
Grasmere LA22 9SW
Tel: 015394 35428

Staff of Life Bakery
2 Berry's Yard
Kendal LA9 4AB
Tel: 01539 738606

Taste!
Rheged
Redhills
Penrith CA11 ODQ
Tel: 01768 860066

The Catch
Maryport Harbour
Maryport CA15 8BW
Tel: 01900 819808

The Village Bakery
Melmerby
Penrith CA10 1HE
Tel: 01768 881811

Westmorland Farm Shops,
M6 Motorway (Northbound and Southbound)
Tebay Service Area
Tel: 015396 24511

NOTE ON ORGANICS

Organic farmers work with nature to ensure healthy soil, crops and livestock by using a combination of methods. Namely rotating crops to replenish nutrients; planting clover crops to add nitrogen to the soil; adding nutrient-rich composts and manure to the soil; keeping animal stocking densities low to avoid overgrazing the lessen the risk of disease; ensuring animal welfare needs are met; and providing suitable habitats for predators such as ladybirds, beetles and birds which help to keep pest species under control.

Organic food is produced without chemical pesticides, fungicides and herbicides. No genetically modified organisms are allowed in seeds, crops, animal feedstuffs and animals.

CONTACT:
The Soil Association, Bristol House, 40 –56 Victoria Street, Bristol BS1 6BY
Telephone: 0117 929 0661 www.soilassociation.org.
Email: info@soilassociation.org

NOTE ON CUMBRIA ORGANICS

Cumbria Organics was set up in 1999 to provide self-help support to the increasing number of local farmers converting to organic production. The group also raises consumer awareness about organic food, helps to develop supply chains and provides technical information for anyone interested in farming to organic standards. Cumbria Organics has about 70 members, almost 30 of whom are selling direct to the public.

CONTACT:
www.cumbriaorganics.org
Joyce Brocklebank - Telephone 01229 716439.
Email: JoyceBram@aol.com

Hadrian Organics was set up in 2003 to enable a small group of organic producers near to Carlisle to market themselves collectively.
CONTACT:
www.hadrianorganics.co.uk
Susan Aglionby, Croft Farm Meats, Houghton, Carlisle, CA3 OLD
Tel: 01228 549628

NOTE ON BIODYNAMICS

The practice of biodynamic farming is as suggested by Rudolf Steiner, who was a scientist and philosopher and who died in 1925. It embraces the idea that the whole earth is a living organism and each farm is a unique individuality within it. Biodynamic farming is self sustaining, depending largely for its manures and feedstuffs on its own resources and thereby benefiting and harmonising with the environment rather than exploiting it. Biodynamic farms are run as mixed farms with an appropriate balance of animals and crops, a system of recycling and benign methods of pest and disease control.
CONTACT
The Biodynamic Agricultural Association, Painswick Inn Project, Gloucester Street, Stroud, GL5 1QG
Telephone: 01453 759501. www.biodynamic.org.uk.
Email: office@biodynamic.org.uk.

NOTE ON SLOW FOOD

Slow Food is the antithesis to fast food. The movement has grown rapidly in the United Kingdom since its beginnings in 1997. There are 25 convivia throughout the UK.
CONTACT for Cumbria
Email: info@slowfoodcumbria.org.uk
Website: www.slowfoodcumbria.org.uk

LIST OF PRODUCERS IN THE TEXT

Acorn Bank, Temple Sowerby, Penrith, Cumbria CA10 1SP
Tel: 017683 61893
Email: acornbank@nationaltrust.org.uk
Website: www.nationaltrust.org.uk

Alfie Bennett - Shrimper
Stoneleigh, Eastcote, Skinburness, Silloth, Cumbria CA7 4 QH
Tel: 016973 32571
www.bennettssolwayshrimp.co.uk

Birdoswald Cheese, Slack House Farm, Gilsland, Brampton, Cumbria CA8 7DB
Eric Horn – Organic Cheese Maker
Tel: 016977 47351.
Email: slackhousefarm@lineone.net
Website: www.slackhousefarm.co.uk

W. Copsey & Sons Ltd, Camerton, Workington, Cumbria CA14 1LP
Tim Copsey – Vegetable Producer
Tel: 01900 602115

Cowmire Hall Damson Gin
Oliver and Vicki Barratt
Cowmire Hall, Crosthwaite, Kendal, Cumbria LA8 8JJ
Tel: 015395 68200
Website: wwwcowmire.hall@ecosse.net

Cream of Cumbria, Howberry, Blackford, Carlisle, Cumbria CA6 4EN
Sue Forrester – Butter Maker
Tel: 01228 675558.
Email: tomsusan@forrester32.fsnet.co.uk

Croft Farm Meats, Houghton, Carlisle, CA3 0LD
Susan Aglionby – Longhorn Cattle producer
Tel: 01228 549628
Email: susan@aglionby.demon.co.uk

Cumbria On A Plate – Gourmet Tours of Cumbria
Annette Gibbons
Tel: 01900 881356
Website: www.cumbriaonaplate.co.uk

Deer 'n Dexter, Old Stoddah Farm, Penruddock, Penrith, Cumbria CA11 0RY
Jane Emerson and Peter Stoeken,
Organic Deer Farmers.
Tel : 01768 480069
Email: jane@deer-n-dexter.co.uk
Website: www.deer-n-dexter.co.uk

Hawkshead Trout Farm, Riding Wood, Ambleside, Hawkshead, Cumbria LA22 0QF
Nigel Woodhouse - Organic Trout Farmer
Tel: 015394 36541
Email: trout@hawkshead.demon.co.uk
www.organicfish.com

Eric A Hope,
Fly casting instructor and fishing guide.
Myrtle Cottage, Newlands Road, Braithwaite, Keswick, Cumbria CA12 5ST
Tel: 017687 78575